TAGHCONIC;

OR

Letters and Legends about our Summer Home.

BY GODFREY GREYLOCK.

"Thou shalt look
Upon the green and rolling forest tops,
And down into the secrets of the glens,
And streams, that with their bordering thickets strive
To hide their windings. Thou shalt gaze at once
Here on white villages and tilth and herds,
And swarming roads, and there on solitudes
That only hear the torrent, and the wind,
And eagles shriek."

BRYANT.

Entered according to Act of Congress, in the year 1852,
BY J. E. A. SMITH,
in the Clerk's Office of the District Court of the District of Massachusetts.

BOSTON:
Stacy and Richardson, Printers,
No. 11 Milk Street.

EPISTLE DEDICATORY

To Summer Ramblers on the Berkshire Hills.

Friends: —

From Vermont upon the north to Connecticut upon the south, for fifty miles along the eastern borders of New York, extends Berkshire, the most western county of Massachusetts. It is a region of hills and valleys, of lake and stream, of woodland, farm and field. Its beauty is world renowned; for the pens of Bryant and Miss Sedgwick have made it their favorite theme. Within its limits are Monument Mountain, Icy Glen, the Stockbridge Bowl, Green River, with a thousand other scenes of storied or of unsung loveliness.

In the north rise majestically, six thousand feet into the air, the double peaks of Greylock. Along our western borders lie the dome like summit of the Taghconic range. Less graceful in outline, but even more romantic with broken and precipitous ascents, the Hoosacs shut out the world upon the east. Within this mountain walled amphitheatre lies cradled the upland valley of the Housatonic, with all its fertile farms, its mansion homes, and frequent villages. Somebody has called it the Piedmont of America. I do not know how just the appellation may be, but I do know that if Piedmont can rightly be called the Berkshire of Europe, it must be a very delightful region.

What we most admire in Berkshire scenery is its freshness, boldness, and variety. Our hills boast no astounding grandeur; there is nothing about them of an Alpine character; they possess few scenes which can properly rank with the sublime. The highest mountain tops, the most precipitous cliffs, — sufficient to claim our admiration, wild enough to be the marvel of tourists from the tame coast country, — cannot, for a moment, compare with similar scenes among the White Mountains, or the Alleghanies — not to mention more unapproachable wonders of Nature. Our deepest ravines, often penetrated by smooth, flower bordered roads, are very different things, indeed, from the earthquake rifted chasms of other lands.

If the traveller seek some object for a day's or a week's wonder, some tremendous cataract or "Heaven piercing Cordillera," he must seek it elsewhere. But if he asks for a retreat among wild and picturesque scenery, adorned by much that is pleasant and refined in his city life, but far removed from its heat and turmoil; where he can draw closer the silken cord of social intercourse, and yet throw loose some of its galling chains; where nature ennobles by her greatness but never chills with a frown, he may find it all amid the varied beauty of the Berkshire Hills.

The inexhaustible variety of our vistas is wonderful. It is marvellous in what an endless series of combinations, mountain, valley, lake, stream, rock, field and wood, present themselves. Wherever you go, you meet a constant succession of changes which at once charm the eye and delight the heart. At every turn

"You stand suddenly astonished,
You are gladdened unaware."

Through the long Summer months you may seek, and not in vain, some new object, daily, of interest and pleasure. But that you will not do; a few spots will become so dear that, while you revisit them again and again, others of perhaps greater merit will remain neglected.

So profusely has Nature scattered her treasures in this fair land, that it is thought by most, superfluous to search out her more choice and hidden gems. Many of the most unique and beautiful of these remained concealed from those who have passed their lives within a rifle shot of them. The traditions which were once attached to almost all these scenes are also rapidly fading away, with the fading years of grey haired men. "There was a story," I have been often told, "Old Deacon Whitehead used to tell, but he is dead and I have forgotten the details."

To make known some of these hidden retreats of beauty, to revive and preserve a few of these half forgotten traditions, was the design with which these brief pages were commenced. It has been a work of greater difficulty than was anticipated, to procure the necessary information, although now, when it is too late to be of service, much new material is offered. It will not be improper, perhaps, to say here, that during our progress, circumstances have occurred which rendered necessary a slight change in the character originally intended, and the omission of a great deal of matter, of merely local interest, which was already written.

And now to you, whom I have presumed to call my friends, and for whom this little volume was more especially designed, I commend, for your kindness, what is done. Every page was written with a sympathy for your admiration of this pleasant county, which expanded as it warmed, into personal friendship for yourselves. If I shall point any of you to scenes of Nature's gladness, to which you would otherwise have been strangers; if I shall contribute one moment of happiness to your Summer hours; if I shall hereafter recall more vividly to your mind these rural scenes, when they shall be a little faded, I shall be amply repaid; how much more, if I shall add one pleasant thought to mingle with your own, as you gaze upon the grand, the noble, or the beautiful, in our dear mountain valley.

GODFREY GREYLOCK.

Pittsfield, September, 1852.

CONTENTS.

TAGHCONIC.

CHAPTER I.

OUR TOWN.—ITS OLD ELM.—ITS ENVIRONS.—ITS PEOPLE.—ITS PAST AND PRESENT.

To be sure the first claim which our town has to notice is that it *is* ours. The "*propriâ*" is an excellent and universally recognised title to our affections; the very idea of property is genial to our hearts—even if it be only in the travelled streets of a town, with so much of Heaven's universal gifts as one can there possess, use and enjoy, in common with six thousand copartners. "Mine" and, more intensely, "mine own" are terms of superlative endearment in the *patois* of the novel writers. So deeply indeed is this correspondence between ownership and affection implanted in the breast, that no sooner does a man conceive a passion for his neighbor's house, horse, or any thing that is his, than an uneasy, feverish desire to transfer the possession betrays that his mind is out of unison with the harmony of Nature. Nowhere is this reciprocal relation more heartily honored than in the love which the good people of PITTSFIELD bear to their beautiful town. Waiving, however, this claim, which is, in its terms, not binding upon a stranger, our town has a title to affectionate admiration in its beauty, its environs and its associations, which no traveller ever desires to impeach. It is indeed a fair town. Standing in the centre of that magnificent panorama of hills which encompasses the County of Berkshire, it is encircled by a chain of beauty. Branching from its central green, delightful avenues extend in all directions into the most picturesque and inviting regions; but, before we permit them to entice us away, let us linger a little while under the circular grove of elms which shades its green.

You must have heard of the Old Elm of Pittsfield; it rises here above us — the scarred and seared veteran of centuries in the midst of the young green growth. Straight into the air it soars one hundred and twenty six feet; a tall, grey pillar, bearing upon its head a few green branches and a few withered, shattered, and bare limbs. From Greylock to Monument Mountain there is no inanimate thing so reverend and venerable as this.

It has had hair-breadth escapes in its day — has that old tree. When it stood a graceful sapling in the untouched forest — wherein as yet no white man had his habitation — it is told that the Indian war parties came hither at night, with the pale-faced prisoners whom they had taken from the Southern settlements. Here, upon the place which is now our peaceful green, they pitched their camp, and bound the swollen and bleeding limbs of their miserable captives to the young elm, while they slept. Once, as the story goes, a prisoner, worn out by the way and unable to proceed, was bound to the lithe trunk of the elm, the faggots piled around him and already lighted, for the last rite of savage cruelty, when Providence interfered — probably in the shape of a French priest, or officer,— the victim was rescued, and with him the young tree escaped its first danger from the hand of man; but the kindling flames had left their mark upon it, by which it was afterwards recognised.

It lived to see the red race vanish from the land, and another people usurp their hunting-grounds; but its own dangers were not yet past. The new race were pious and Godly men, and must have a temple in which to worship the Most High. They built themselves a Meeting-house — which we may suppose to have been a rude and simple structure — close by the Elm. A few years passed, they grew mightily, and their borders became too narrow for them. It was determined to build a larger and more goodly church. Meanwhile the Elm had grown very tall and straight, and the devout deacons who had it in charge to build the new sanctuary, cast their eyes upon it and said that it was convenient and fitting for a principal beam in the frame. Perhaps they thought the Almighty had planted and preserved it there for that special purpose, as He once furnished a ram to Abraham for a sacrifice. If any such thought did enter their hearts the event proved its falsity; the tree turned out the better representative of Isaac,—for at the critical moment, when it was about to be sacrificed, an angel appeared to save it, in the person of one Mrs. Williams, a brave and excellent dame who lived not far off. Seeing the preparations for felling her favorite tree, she placed herself as a shield before it, and so stoutly maintained her post that the destroyers were at last either softened or shamed from their purpose, and the tree was permitted to remain.

The husband of this brave and gentle lady did his share toward the preservation of the Old Elm. On Sundays the devout worshippers were in the habit of fastening their horses to iron spikes, with which they had encircled the tree; the sermons, in those days, were none of the shortest, and while their masters waited for the third turning of the hour-glass, the beasts made ruinous havoc with the bark and roots of the Elm. To prevent this weekly equine attack, Mr. Williams piled up a barricade of stones, which proved an effective protection. It is to this gentleman that the village owes also its public square, — of which he gave the southern half from his own land, on condition that the town should place their Meeting-house at a corresponding distance from the Elm on the north.

The tree, having survived the attacks of savage and civilized man, had a more formidable enemy to encounter. Some years ago, a thunder-bolt fell upon it, and running down its side stripped away the bark, leaving a naked wound of ghastly whiteness, from top to bottom. The fiery fluid dried up the juices in its old veins; many of the limbs died, and the whole tree, surviving the fury of savage and the piety of civilized man, is slowly perishing of the wrath of Heaven. A few branches yet flourish greenly, but year by year grow less. It is evident our old friend will survive not many more Winters; and as often as the Spring begins to swell the buds in the grove, the question is asked anxiously, "Will the Old Elm survive this year, also?"

Yet even in its death it is fortunate; the long, white streak, where the scathing lightning passed adown its trunk, caught the eye of Herman Mellville, who interwove it with his strong-lined portrait of Captain Ahab. "Threading its way," he says, "out from among his grey hairs, and continuing right down one side his tawny, scorched face and neck, till it disappeared in his clothing, you saw a slender, rod-like mark, lividly whitish. It resembled that perpendicular seam sometimes made in the straight, lofty trunk of a great tree, when the upper lightning tearingly darts down it, and, without wrenching a single twig, peels and grooves out the bark, from top to bottom, ere running off into the soil, — leaving the tree still greenly alive, but branded." There you have a graphic picture of one of the most noticeable features of our Old Elm; and thus, in its death stroke it received a new life, — as the ancients fabled that they who died by the lightning's bolt, thereby became immortal.

Branching from the central square, extend the broad, quiet, shaded streets, bordered by pretty white-walled houses, with handsome gardens and court-yards green with shrubbery, — a delightful Summer promenade. To the town's people these dwellings are each pregnant with associations of the past; each has its story. They tell you — these good citizens — as you pass along, now pleasant, gossiping histories; now low hissed scandals, mouldy and soured, which ought long ago to have been in their graves; and occasionally you hear a tale of open or proved guilt, such as you would rather not

1*

believe could have its dwelling in such innocent-looking homes. Yet is our town unsurpassed, in the virtue, intelligence, and cultivation of its citizens. One who calls it "ours" only by courtesy can modestly say it.

You hear them speak names which call up no image in your mind, and which have long since ceased to receive an answer in these streets. They call places by appellations unfamiliar to your ears. The iron horse has brought new wealth, prosperity and hope to the thriving town. There are groceries where there used to be gardens; mansions where there used to be meadows. The town is richer and handsomer than it was; but in many hearts, for whom the old quiet used to be full of joy and peace, the new wealth and crowd and noisy prosperity cannot but sometimes awaken painful longings. In the stillness of the evening — when the shrill cry of the steam-whistle pierces the ear and goes echoing into the breathless distance, like the shout of a drunken man on the solemn midnight — you listen to their touching reminiscences of the past, and are moved by laments for which the eager, throbbing heart of common life has no chord in unison.

In these streets live some whose names are known to fame. A little apart from the village is the mansion and farm of Governor BRIGGS — our model man. The mansion is a handsome one, in a fine location, and profusely surrounded with shrubbery. Nearer our square is the residence of the Rev. Dr. TODD. To say nothing of his eloquence as a divine, and his excellence as a writer of light literature, every student ought to make a pilgrimage to the home of the author of the "Student's Manual," — the most perfect work of its kind ever written; to whose paternal and skillful advice many young men owe all they are or will be.

On a gentle knoll on one of our most beautiful streets, is the country seat of Hon. NATHAN APPLETON, in which is the "Old Clock on the Stairs," celebrated by Professor LONGFELLOW.

"Somewhat back from the village street
Stands the old fashioned country seat;
Across its antique portico
Tall poplar trees their shadows throw, —
And from its station in the hall
An ancient time-piece says to all —
Forever, never,
Never, forever."

A couple of miles farther south, upon a little hill, around which the Housatonic makes a graceful curve, is the villa of OLIVER WENDELL HOLMES. His estate here is the relic of a whole township, purchased of the Indians by an ancestor of the poet. He thus tells the story in a speech at the Berkshire Jubilee, in 1848. "In the year 1735, Hon. Jacob Wendell, my grandfather in the maternal line, bought a township, not then laid out — the township of Pontoosuc, (now Pittsfield,) — and that little spot which we still hold is the relic of 24,000 acres of baronial territory. When I say this, no feeling which can be the subject of ridicule animates my bosom; I know too well that the hills and rocks outlast our families; I know that we fall upon the places we claim as the leaves of the forest fall, — and, as passed the soil from the original occupants into the hands of my immediate ancestor, I know it must pass from me and mine; and yet, with pleasure and pride I feel that I can take every inhabitant by the hand and say, that if not a son nor a grandson of this fair county, I am at least allied by an hereditary relation."

Adjoining the estate of Dr. Holmes is that of HERMAN MELLVILLE, who has retired thus far from the sea, where nothing can remind him of the familiar sounds of Ocean, save the roar of the wind among the forest trees.

"Oh, home returned, what joy to tell
Of all the dangers that befell
The sailor boy at sea."

These gentlemen come hither for quiet; let us leave them to it, hoping that they may find in the bracing mountain air inspiration for a hundred things as wise and witty as "Astrea," and as enchantingly truthful as "Typee."

For ourselves, we will close our ramble round the town by climbing South Mountain — a favorite resort of the town's people. Few spots any where are more attractive. Passing from its foot, up the broad, natural terraces which wind around it, bordered by a thousand variegated wild flowers, to its rocky summit, you are presented with scenes of ever-changing beauty. The over-view from the summit is the best you can find of Pittsfield and the northern valley, as far as Greylock. Standing on its topmost rock, under a spreading oak which waves its branches like a green banner, high above the surrounding wood, you will be enchanted by the varied scene below.

Just at your feet, in the lands of J. R. MOREWOOD, Esq., will lie the Mellville Pond — the tiniest little lakelet you ever saw, — so crystal, clear, and pure, that a fanciful and poetic friend calls it a "Tear of Heaven." There is a cool and mossy path upon its eastern border, completely overarched by trees, — "No more sky, for overbranching at your head than at your feet." Rarely, through a leaf-screened crevice, the green and golden light streams down with a subdued gorgeousness. There is something exquisitely rich in these and other woodland tints; I cannot forget the purple hue which a few struggling rays of light imparted to a little spot of black earth, as I walked in this cool retreat once when it was fierce noontide without. The very outlines marked by its rich, deep coloring, are vividly present to me now; while so much that seemed more enduring has faded from existence, and is fading from memory.

But back again to our mountain top. It is the smallest of three sister hills; on its western side is Mt. Oceola — another much prized resort, but of less gentle attractions than South Mountain. Still farther to the west is Perry's Peak; I have never visited it, but am told the view from it is hardly, if at all, surpassed by that from Greylock, and I can well believe it.

Other beautiful things are shown to us from this pinnacle, but of them anon; other things of interest might be said of our people, but of that also at another, perhaps a distant time.

CHAPTER II.

WASHINGTON MOUNTAIN. — UNDINE'S GLEN. AND LAKE ASHLEY.

THIS last has been a week of rare sultriness with us — the fierce, dying flicker of Summer's life flame. The maple leaves have lost the last remnant of their glossy freshness; the cattle stand cooling themselves under the willow trees in the still pools of the river; long ago the birds ceased their songs and fled into the deeper recesses of the woods; we human idlers lie listlessly under the shade of the nearer groves, in dreamy reveries or feeble speculations upon the probable destiny of some little cloud which may chance to speck the horizon — the forlorn hope of a thunder-shower. At evening we broach some mild beverage of conversation, but if any venturous tongue leads the imagination to your torrid city of Manhattoes, we start back as if from the flaming mouth of a furnace. On the most fiery day of this fiery seven, came a friend who, that day of all others, must climb Washington Mountain. No flaming sword of the elements could deter him, and all the chivalry of friendship forbade me to abandon his side. This Washington Mountain is part of the Hoosac range, a continuation of the Green Mountains, which runs through the entire length of Berkshire County, on its eastern border. The point which we were to visit lies some seven miles east of Pittsfield, and seven hundred feet above it; that is, not far from eighteen hundred feet above tide-water, at Albany.

Thinking to escape the more violent heat, we set out at a very early hour, but the air was already intensely sultry, and, still worse, was filled with a fine white dust, that completely penetrated eyes, nose, and mouth. We could neither see, breathe, nor speak, with comfort; and the gritty particles between our teeth sent a nervous shudder through the whole frame. As we ascended the mountain we came upon a fine breeze which never fails there, and which at the same time aggravated the plague of the dust, and inspired us with vigor to devise and execute a remedy.

Ever and anon, by the road-side, appeared glimpses of a deep, rocky gorge. Up this, L. proposed to ascend the mountain by a path familiar to him, and, accordingly, sending our horse forward, we plunged down a steep descent thick beset with brambles. At the bottom, a little brook came tumbling and purling down the hill, and, yielding to its suggestions, we indulged in a series of luscious ablutions. None but those who have experienced the like, can know the thrilling vigor and elasticity which penetrated us with the cool mountain air when the burning and inflammatory dust was once removed from the pores.

Filled with new life, we pushed eagerly up the brook, now clambering over huge angular blocks of flint rock, now sauntering along smooth patches of green sward, and anon pushing our way through a thorny hedge of blackberry bushes, hanging full of the ripest fruit.

Still L. led on, till we came to a little level spot of green sward, around which the brook swept in a graceful curve, while a thick leaved maple overhung it. We were here shut out from all sight of human habitation. The only traces of man's ravages were the weather-beaten stumps, which stood, ghastly memorials of his parricidal war with nature, like the bleached sculls which the ploughman turns up on an ancient battle-field. The precipitous hills, on either side, were yet shaggy, although not as of old, with the maple, the beech, the fir, and the hemlock. Just up the gorge, the streamlet leaped down a black ledge in a silver white column; while, beyond, the glen was dark with narrowing cliffs and over-hanging trees. Bravely, but in vain, the gorgeous sunshine darted its arrowy rays into that Thermopylæ of gloom.

L. flung himself at full length beneath the maple, and I was glad to follow his example. "Do you know," he said, "this is Undine's Glen? Shall I tell you the story of how it got its foreign name?" Do, I replied.

Undine's Gorge.

One day in June, some ten years ago, there came to the village hotel in P. two ladies; the one, Miss Helen V., an heiress, and what was more, a spirited, brilliant, and natural girl. The other was her maiden aunt, Miss M., neither young nor pretty, yet a little romantic and not a little stiff in her manners. Miss M. held moreover the responsible office of guardian to her niece, which that young lady took the best care should be anything but a sinecure.

Riding, walking, and reading, the lone dames whiled away a week or two; when, provokingly enough, just as the last page of their last light reading was cut, there came a rainy, dreary day, as such days will come, even in June. At such desperate junctures, solid literature and re-readings are not to be thought of; so recourse was had to the landlord. That functionary was anxious to serve his fair guests, but unfortunately his shelves contained just what they had already read. Suddenly his face brightened with a new idea. Among his boarders was one Dr. M., who, to enliven his hours in the country had brought with him from New York a curious library. This gentleman was summoned, and made his appearance, — a very personable young gentleman and a clever. The wants of the ladies were made known to him, and he invited them to examine his library for themselves, and some pictures which he prized as well.

Helen was delighted, although she did not exactly say so then; Miss M. hesitated, with some secret misgivings, but finally, overcome by the fiend ennui and the frank bearing of M., she, courteously enough, accepted the invitation. Evening was upon them before they had completed the survey, for, besides his paintings by other artists, M. modestly displayed his own portfolio, filled with sketches of foreign as well as neighboring scenery. Helen eagerly turned them over, and M. had an enthusiastic word for many a remembered scene. After Miss M. had several times reminded her of her prolonged stay, Helen selected De La Motte Fouque's delightful romance of "Undine" from the library, and that evening M. read it aloud to them in their parlor. Before they parted the ladies had consented to accompany him on the morrow to this spot, of which he was going to complete a sketch. So does friendship ripen when the right sun-light falls upon it.

They came hither; the artist fixed his easel and wrought on his sketch. Helen, seated at the foot of this maple, read "Undine" to her aunt. But both found an interval to wander up the glen; so with reading, sketching, romancing, — and most likely eating — the day wore away and the night came, — a moonlight night and a moonlight ride home.

Some days passed, in which M. gained hugely in the good opinion of his fair friends, who continually teased him for a sight of his sketch — which he declared should not be seen until it was completed. Thus something of an air of mystery had woven itself around the picture when at last he brought it out, altogether with the air of a man who knows he has done a nice thing, and is rather proud to have the world see it.

Never was pride more completely dashed, or lover more completely puzzled. Helen blushed and smiled, but looked strangely and heartily vexed. The guardian aunt frowned unequivocally — not to say scowled. Poor M. turned from one to the other in most innocent and ludicrous bewilderment; but finally settled down into a fixed consideration of the cloud which had so suddenly gathered on the old lady's brow, — as a Summer storm sometimes will over the placid surface of Lake Ashley. The Summer storm is transient, but Miss M. seemed to have an inexhaustible magazine of wrath behind her wrinkled forehead. So, taking a hint from Helen's eye, at the first growl of the thunder M. fled.

The tempest was brewed in this wise. The good old lady, with all her romance and stateliness, had a spice of puritanism about her, and the special phase in which it shewed itself was a prudish modesty in the matter of pictures. Why it took this form, more than any other, might be discovered, perhaps, if we could pry into the crooks and crannies of her early history. At present it only concerns us to know that it was there, and that in consequence of it she issued a husky edict for M. to "take his vile picture hence."

Now this vile painting was neither more nor less than a simple and spirited sketch of this scene, into which the artist had interwoven a portrait of Helen in the character of Undine. All very well — only the painter, with the modest assurance of his art, had changed the maiden's chaste garb for a bit of flimsy drapery, which displayed the ivory neck and swelling bosom, the taper leg and rosy foot, as circumstantially as though he had had the original all the while before him for a model. O fair and false imagination, to steal away so fair and true a reality!

Miss M. would have thought her ward's character altogether compromised by interchanging a word more with the immoral young man M. had proved himself, in her estimation. Helen thought quite otherwise. Fortunately for M., there was another difference in their notions. The aunt loved her morning pillow — the niece her morning walk, — and this taste of the damsel's now acquired a new strength that would have charmed Dr. Alcott. In another point of view these sunrise excursions to South Mountain and Mellville's Lake might have been thought alarmingly frequent. The young lady could not have been expected or desired to make her walks solitary, but one who saw how demurely they met at the breakfast table would not have surmised that the painter had been her companion an hour before.

But the end was not yet; walking, it seems, would not content them,— they must ride as well. So one balmy morning in the grey twilight, a pair of spirited greys were reined up at the south door of the Berkshire House, while our young friends took their places behind them; and then heigho for Lebanon! "They 'll have fleet steeds that follow, quoth young Lochinvar." Gallant champions of Love, these same fiery greys! Before then and since they have borne beating hearts up the hills and down the valleys of that seven miles of Hymen's highway which lie between the jurisdiction of the puritan publishment laws and the marriage encouraging State of New York. I wonder if any where in this western world more visions of happiness have been dreamed, more passionate pulsations throbbed, than between the tall Elm of Pittsfield and the all-curing Springs of Lebanon. The very murmurs of the groves have caught the soft tones of lover's vows; the sparkling streams reflect the ardent gleam of expectant bridegroom's eyes.

Over this hymenial highway that balmy morning our happy couple were rapidly whirled, and before the sun was up, the words were said which bound them in that union which no words can unloose. I doubt if their steeds were urged as impatiently on their return, but they reached their hotel again while the careless guardian, fatigued with the last night's novel, yet slept. How they ever reconciled matters with her I never heard; but it was done, for last week she sat quietly by, while M., in a little recessed back parlor in Brooklyn, told me the story of his wooing. On the wall, too, he pointed out to me the identical "vile painting;" and by her mother's side a little Undine of eight Summers shook her sunny curls and laughed. I do n't think the painter ever regretted his day's sketching in the wild glen he christened "Undine's Gorge."

The story told, and a bumper drained to the health of the heroine,—again up, still up the cool gorge, till it diverged to the north, while our path lay southward Reclaiming our team, we now soon reached the summit and looked down upon the wild, billowy sea of mountains, which stretched far away to the north-east,—a taller peak sometimes dashing its splintered crest into the air, and a white village spire or a red farm-house appearing here and there a floating waif upon the waste. Upon a lofty point, miles away, sat the pretty village of Middlefield, glittering in the sun-light and looking like a white walled Moorish town among the Alpuxuras.

Turning away at last from this majestic overview, we passed down a rustic road which leads to the south, and were soon riding along the borders of Lake Ashley—a little romantic loch which lies upon the summit of the mountain. It is indeed a most exquisite sheet of water. Nothing can exceed the cold, pure serenity of its dark waves. Lined on all sides but one by unbroken woods, fed only by fountains which gush from below, with neither speck nor boat on all its tranquil surface, it seemed, as we rode slowly along its eastern border, the waters of solitude. It should be so; for since the Indians' graceful bark is gone forever, there remains none which would not do violence to the lonely beauty of the scene. We call it Lake Ashley — a pretty name enough, but none worthy of it could come except from an Indian imagination and in the soft syllables of the native tongue, like those in which that more magnificent mountain lake was called Winnee-pissaukee — (not Winnepiseoga) — the smile of GOD.

In long, delicious draughts we drank deep to the mountain maids and the maids of the valley, — to the spirits of air, earth, and water, — not forgetting those enterprising gentlemen who propose to lead these waters from their aerie home to the doors of the people of Pittsfield. To these gentlemen, and through them to Dr. Jackson, I am indebted for the assurance that this water is as pure as it seems to be — that is, the nearest natural approach to distilled water.

East of the Lake, a little round well-wooded noppit rises, and ascending it we found a bed of very pure and beautiful granular quartz, which used to be worked for the use of the eastern glass manufacturers, but is long since abandoned, on account of the far greater abundance, as well as facilities for transportation and working, in other localities.

Upon the northern side of the noppit is piled a rugged heap of those flint boulders, so frequent in this region. A few curious lichens grow upon them, and in the crevices some beautiful wild flowers. Taking specimens of these, as well as the quartz, and drinking one farewell draught at the Lake, we began our return.

As we descended, a succession of fine views of the valley of the Housatonic presented themselves. Now the cultivated interval, then the green hills of Taghconic, and still beyond the blue and cloud-like summits of the Kaatskills.

It is from this hill some of the most beautiful effects of atmospheric changes are observed, — and here the sea of mist filling the valley and then rolling up its sides, like the breaking up of the great deep, astonishes the gazer. A gentleman tells me that travellers, after having the road to Pittsfield pointed out to them, often inquire how they are to cross the Lake — so completely deceptive is the veil of mist.

CHAPTER III.

ROARING BROOK. — TORIES' GLEN. — AND SOMETHING ABOUT THE TORIES.

"EVERY State and almost every county of New England has its Roaring Brook — a mountain streamlet, overhung by woods, impeded by a mill, encumbered by fallen trees, but ever rushing, racing, roaring down through gurgling gullies and filling the forest with its delicious sound and freshness; the drinking places of home returning herds; the mysterious haunts of squirrels and blue jays; the sylvan retreat of school boys, who frequent it in the Summer holidays and mingle their restless thoughts with its restless, exuberant, and rejoicing stream."

Thus speaks Professor Longfellow, of one of the prettiest elements in our native scenery. Our Roaring Brook I think must be familiar to the poet. Indeed, it is shrewdly suspected that it is the original of that where Churchill and Kavanagh passed so delightful a day with Cecilia, Alice, and the schoolmaster's wife; if not, it might very well have been.

Issuing from Lake Ashley, it comes leaping and dashing down the deep and rocky ravine, smiling in sunshine and glooming in shade, — all the while roaring in a way fully to justify its noisy cognomen, —

although I cannot help thinking that it would be more poetic to call it the "Lion Brook," which would include in the metaphor its shaggy mane of forest trees, and the gaping jaws of the gorge, — which, by the bye, we once christened the "jaws of darkness," to the fierce indignation of a fair friend.

One warm October day, a three mile walk brought us to a smiling and fertile valley, which lies just without the mouth of the Tories' Gorge, through which our Roaring Brook comes tumbling down. We were charmed by the cheerful aspect of the farm-houses, which were here gathered into a neat and handsome hamlet. From the courteous and intelligent manner of the people, we were not surprised to learn that their village was within the limits of the town of Lenox. So gaily the sunshine fell upon the shorn fields, so cheerily the husbandmen were employed in completing their harvesting, and such a genial spirit of plenty seemed to pervade the whole scene, that we were tempted to commit the sentimental folly of calling it the "happy valley."

Following a bye-path kindly pointed out to us, and guided by the sounds of the Brook, we soon entered the dark shades of the gorge, through which it comes leaping impatiently from fall to fall, for five weary miles, until it loses itself in the winding Housatonic. It must be a sweet relief to the water — vexed and wearied by its rough passage among the sharp angled flint rocks, and by its arduous labors in turning mill wheels — thus to repose at length in the flower bordered bed of the river, and wander about the meadows, in what leisurely and graceful curves it will.

The change from the cheerful light of the hamlet to the wild and beautiful solitude within the gorge, is strikingly impressive. From the shadeless field you enter upon overarched paths, — among mossy trees, tall, precipitous cliffs, and broken, topling crags. The heart feels the change instantly, and conforms itself instinctively to it.

Here we find those adamantine blocks of flint-rock which characterize and rudely adorn this whole mountain range. Sometimes they lie confusedly upon the mountain's steep slope, then again they impede the rushing course of the brook. In the bed of the stream the ever-rolling current, in the course of ages, has polished and rounded even these obdurate masses. It is startling to think by how many years of constant attrition the soft flowing wave has accomplished its purpose. How many centuries ago did the savage stoop to drink at this mountain stream, and think of nothing but the cooling draught — least of all that the smooth, gliding fluid was bearing away a portion of the solid rock whereon he stood, to form a soil for a conquering race! Yet here, two thousand years ago, Nature kept some million tons of water at work, to add a few ounces in the year to what should be the farm of her true worshipper — Oliver Wendell Holmes. Meanwhile the poet's ancestors were roasting people at Stonehenge, by great baskets'-full, — far less mindful than Mother Nature of their witty and polished descendant.

Upon either side the ravine these rocks are piled up on the hill sides in the maddest confusion, — with crevices and dens between and beneath them, which in former days may have afforded accommodation for a whole city of wild beasts. I wearied myself with seeking among them for one cavern, which tradition says in revolutionary times afforded shelter to the hunted Tories. I might have saved myself some trouble and chagrin, by paying closer attention to my directions, for I could not satisfy myself of its locality, and was afterwards informed that it is not on the hill-side at all, but under the road over which I passed, — and although likely to escape observation, perfectly easy of access when you once know the way.

One of the Tories — thus driven out to make their homes among wild beasts — must nevertheless have been a kind man at heart. They tell a touching incident of him, that, when concealed in some hiding place at home, he made his wife cause all his children to pass daily before a crevice, which supplied him with light and air, that he might see their innocent faces, and know that no harm had befallen them.

With all the harshness which it was deemed necessary by the Whigs to visit upon them, and with all the odium which still clings to their memory, I cannot help thinking that many of the loyalists were good, well-meaning, God-fearing men,— although we cannot doubt that the majority were moved by craven and selfish considerations, and that all were miserably mistaken. It is a mistake very easily discovered now.

Some of the anecdotes which remain of the Tories, among our Berkshire traditions, are very honorable to their character as men. There are two, which I heard from two of our most eminent and learned citizens, and which they received from the best authority — I believe from the late venerable Judge Walker — which are so well authenticated and so characteristic that I shall tell them both — although the latter I think I saw, many years ago, in print — and with a few variations, in unimportant particulars.

In the early part of the Revolution there lived in Lenox a staunch old Tory, who openly professed his allegiance to King George, and his hostility to the rebel cause; but, as he confined his opposition to words, and was greatly respected and beloved by his fellow citizens, for his many excellent qualities as a friend and neighbor, he was allowed for a long while to enjoy his opinions unmolested. But the contest between England and the Colonies waxed every day more bitter, and the Committee of Safety began to be troubled with doubts if it were consistent with their duty to permit one who so loudly vaunted his toryism to live among them, and encourage others to commit outrages of which he would not be personally guilty.

The matter was often a subject of deliberation, but the committee were reluctant to act. At length, however, in some dark and trying hour, — perhaps in the bitterness of defeat, perhaps after hearing of the horrors of Wyoming — they resolved to move. Paying a visit at once to the Tory, they informed him they had come to the conclusion that his example was too pernicious to the cause of Liberty to be any longer permitted. They regretted the circumstance, but their duty was imperative; in short, he must take the oath of allegiance to the Colonies — or swing.

The oath was peremptorily and unhesitatingly refused; and the next step was an extemporaneous gallows, erected in the public street, beneath which the recusant was placed, and the rope tightened around his throat, but immediately loosened and the oath again proffered, and again declined.

All arguments and threats proving abortive, the contemptuous loyalist was again drawn up, and left to hang until he became purple in the face, — care being taken to lower him and apply restoratives, before life was extinct. Consciousness being once more restored, the oath was again tendered, and he was entreated to yield to the necessity of the case, but his stubborn spirit was not yet broken; he refused to renounce his allegiance to the Crown.

Things were now coming to a crisis; the committee, who probably were by this time sorry they had taken the matter in hand, retired for consultation. It was resolved that, to retreat after going so far as they had done, would weaken their authority, and that the good of the cause required that the prisoner should take the oath, or suffer death for his contumacy.

The loyalist received their decision with unflinching determination not to yield a hair's breadth in what he believed to be the right. The committee were equally resolved, and he was again drawn up, — perhaps with some angry violence. At once the limbs stiffened; the arms hung down; it seemed the work of death was too faithfully done. Probably the committee had not intended to carry the matter to such an extreme; if they did, such a sight might well have brought back their old affection for a tried friend and kind neighbor. They hastened to cut down the body, and use every effort to undo their fatal work.

There seemed at first little hope of reanimating the

senseless clay; but at length the limbs slightly relaxed their rigidity, the eyes moved, and the livid hue began to disappear from the cheek. Consciousness slowly and painfully returned; the victim sat upright, — and the question was again asked: "Will you swear?" "Yes," faintly responded the half-dead convert to patriotism.

A few moments afterwards, as he was sitting before the tavern fire, warming his limbs chilled by so dangerous an approach to the "icy realm," he was heard to mutter, thoughtfully to himself, — "Well! this is a hard way to make Whigs — but *it 'll do it!*"

And accordingly, from that day to the close of the war, he was one of the most zealous and unwavering of the patriots.

The other anecdote illustrates still more remarkably the same trait of unflinching regard to rectitude.

It seems that at some time during the Revolution one Gideon Smith, of Tyringham — a romantic and beautiful town in the south of Berkshire — was accused of the crime of high treason, of which there could be no doubt he was guilty. The trial was to be at Springfield, but the court did not sit for some weeks, — during which interval Smith was confined in the Berkshire County gaol,— but, unwilling to waste the time in idleness, he applied to the Sheriff for permission to go out daily to work, promising to return faithfully to the prison every night. So well was the Tory's character for integrity established, that, although he was committed on a capital charge, and did not deny the facts alleged against him, the Sheriff did not hesitate to comply with his request; and so well was that confidence deserved, that the prisoner never failed to return to his quarters punctually every night, to be locked up.

What follows is a still stronger proof of the reliance placed upon his word. The court was to be held at Springfield, and the journey to it was then a weary one, over rough forest roads. Smith was the only prisoner to be carried on, and the Sheriff complained bitterly of the trouble to which he was subjected, particularly at this busy season of the year. The Tory told him that it was quite unnecessary for him to go — he could go just as well by himself; and again he was trusted, and set out alone and on foot, to go fifty miles through the woods to surrender himself to be tried for his life, upon a charge where he could not hope for an acquital, and by a tribunal whose right to judge him he denied. Surely, if ever a man had an excuse to palliate a violation of confidence, it was he; the idea, however, seems never to have occurred to him.

Luckily for him, on his way he was overtaken by the Hon. Mr. Edwards, then a member of the executive council, to attend a session of which body he was then on his way to Boston. This gentleman entered into conversation with Smith, and, without disclosing his own name or official position, learned the nature of his companion's journey, and something of his history. Pondering upon what he had heard, Mr. Edwards pursued his way to Boston; and Smith, trudging on, soon reached Springfield, and surrendered himself, — was tried; did not deny the facts alleged against him, and, as a matter of course, was found guilty and condemned to death.

In due course the petitions for the pardon of persons under sentence of death were considered by the Honorable Council. After all had been read, Mr. Edwards asked if none had been received in favor of one Gideon Smith, of Tyringham. The reply was that there was none; and a member of the council, who had been present at the trial, remarked that the case was one of such undoubted and aggravated guilt, and the attachment of the criminal to the King's cause so inveterate, that there could be no reason for granting a pardon in this case, unless it was extended in every other.

Mr. Edwards, in reply, related his adventure with Smith on the road, and also his story, which he had taken pains to have substantiated by the Sheriff of Berkshire. A murmur of admiration went round the council board; it was unanimously agreed that such a man ought not to die upon the gallows, and after some brief discussion, an unconditional pardon was made out and dispatched to Springfield.

The number of Tories in this region is said to have been much greater than I used to suppose. The gorges in the Taghconic range, between Hancock and Lanesboro', were favorite rendezvous with them. Previous to one battle — I think that of Bennington — just one half of one company deserted the Continental standard and joined the enemy. Probably they considered their position, after the engagement, more astonishing than agreeable.

Yet, as I said, the anecdotes just repeated show, what common sense would lead us to expect, that there were good men and well-wishers to their country in the loyalist ranks. The worst cause is never without good men among its partizans, nor the best without bad. It must be so while reason dwells side by side in the soul with prejudice.

When sides had once been taken, in the dim light of the dawning struggle the rights and wrongs of things did not so clearly appear to men, blinded by the heat of passion, as to us in the calmness of after years, and with all the light of experience. Besides, powerful motives — too little taken into account in the great aggregate — influence individual minds with irresistible force. One is descended from a long line of loyal ancestors, and the idea is interwoven with his whole life that his first duty to God and man is to maintain the family honor untarnished by rebellion. It may be a false, very false notion, but it has had its thousand martyrs in other days. Another has received some loyal boon that binds him — if of a generous nature — for ever to the cause of the giver. Another was taught by a long lost mother to fear God and honor the King; and still he hears her gentle accents repeat the time-honored prayer, "God save the King."

These may be thought weak and unworthy motives, to be weighed in the balance against a nation's welfare, yet they did exist, and we cannot altogether despise or hate those who, in obedience to them, took part even against our own liberty, and bore the loathed name of Tory.

CHAPTER IV.

PONTOOSUC LAKE AND ROLLING ROCK.

O THOU most rare day in June, whose rain of golden moments fell so preciously by the green borders of Pontoosuc! There shall be few like thee, in the gladdest Summer month!

With L. and two other friends from the dear Tri-Mountain city, I went that faultless morning to pass the "lee lang Simmer day" by the clear waters of our favorite mountain lake,—the popular favorite, for, fair as it is, I confess that it has one rival in my own breast. But this is beautiful enough to satisfy any desire. There can be no finer approach to a fine scene than that by which you reach Pontoosuc,—of which, by the bye, the true Indian name was Schoon-keek-moon-keek. Passing the neat and tasteful manufacturing village, you enter a piece of winding willow-shaded road, on the left of which the ground descends steeply to the rocky bed of the river, which a few rods further on falls in a cataract, whose worst fault is that it is artificial. One not too finically fastidious might find it worthy a moment's notice.

Then comes the blue surface of the lake, in mirror like smoothness, or sparkling in light,—broken only by a pair of emerald islets. You catch your first view of the water between hills covered with a magnificent growth of pine; with, upon one side, here and there an elm and beech. As you pass through these woody portals, the view expands; the farther shore of the lake rises gradually into hills, until afar off in the west it terminates in the graceful Taghconics, — every summit of which, on a calm, clear day, is mirrored undistorted in the unruffled water. On the north the long valley stretches away until it finds its barriers in the double peaks of Greylock. You will pause, as we did, by the two trees which stand in brotherly union on the green lawn-like slope of the eastern bank of the lake, and admire the almost artistic arrangement of the stately grove of pines, the single elm, and the twin oaks and hemlocks.

Driving slowly along the road, with the gently rippling waters upon our left, and the cool evergreen grove upon our right, we stopped here and there, to gather splendid bouquets of the scarlet columbine, and to listen to the chorus of the birds, that joined with most melodious energy in the songs of M. and F.

At the end of the lake, sending our carriage before, we retraced our steps, lingering by the pebbly shore to listen to the little dashings of the wavelets, which simultaneously reminded us all of the beatings of the great billows on the rocky Atlantic shore, one other Summer day. It was singular, this mimicking of the great sea by the little mountain loch. F. said it reminded her how she was once startled by recognising the tones of a distinguished orator in the lispings of his infant grandson.

As we stood here, we espied across the water a tiny

grove, well known to all our lovers of pic-nic. This we determined to honor by making it our bower for the morning, and we soon established ourselves under its shade, with L.'s flute, F.'s guitar, and a plentiful supply of creature comforts. There, with music, poetry, dining, and more indefinable pleasures, we passed five hours, which are not lightly to be forgotten in lives which have few such. I need not describe to you all our lake side joys. Go thither upon such a day and in such company, and, if you do not find them out, never go again.

There are fanciful legends about this lake; one of which is admirably told by Rev. Dr. Todd. There is a superstitious tale, also, that a shadowy bark with a shadowy boatman is sometimes seen to glide over its midnight waters, darting from point to point, as if in search of that which it is doomed never to find. What it is this restless phantom seeks — whether lost love or hidden foe, I do not think that legends tell. I have often passed that way at the "witching hour of night;" some times when the pale moonbeams threw their ghastly light all over the waters, and shrieks and howls were heard, which it was past my zoölogy to assign to any beast, bird, or reptile, — sometimes when the fishing skiffs, with the red glare of their torches, looked sufficiently infernal, — but, for the phantom boatman, I cannot rightly say I ever caught sight of his ghostship.

When the day had a little declined, we resolved to extend our excursion. A mile or so to the north there is a very extraordinary natural curiosity. In a grove upon the land of Socrates Squires, Esq., is a large egg shaped stone, weighing many tons. This titanic mass is so nicely balanced upon a pivot of a few inches width, that, although to the eye one side appears more than doubly to outbalance the other, through all convulsions and commotions of Nature, it remains unmoved and immovable. How this singular rock came perched in its present position, and how it maintains its equilibrium, there must remain a secret. The wise ones guess it to be a relic of the Flood, but are divided in opinion whether the rushing waters found it in its present position and merely washed away the surrounding earth, or whether they tore it from some distant native bed, and set it up here as a trophy of their victorious career. There were too many matters of absorbing interest pressing upon the people of that day, for them to take note even of so extraordinary a pebble as this. There is a tradition extant that this was used by the aborigines for one of their sacrifice rocks. — I do not know upon what authority it rests, but it is well enough to believe it, if you can. One thing is certain, the anomalous nature of this rock never disturbed their simple meditations; they had a ready solution for all such problems, — it was the work of the Great Spirit.

To this singular rock we came, on that beautiful afternoon in June. Passing again the lake side, we turned off by a cross road towards the west, and rolled through a quiet, rural country, whose fields and cattle, even where houses and barns, seemed as much in exuberant enjoyment of the day as ourselves.

> "Every clod feels a stir of might,—
> An instinct within it that reaches and towers,
> And, grasping blindly above it for light,
> Climbs to a soul in grass and flowers;

> The flash of life may well be seen
>   Thrilling back, over hills and valleys;
> The cowslip startles in meadows green;
>   The buttercup catches the sun in its chalice,
> And there 's never a leaf or a bud too mean
>   To be some happy creature's palace."
>
> LOWELL.

We found a splendid view in various directions, from a hill on this road. The Lake has a wilder picturesqueness from this point than from any other, and the view in front of the Taghconics is very fine.

When the sun wanted an hour of his setting, we passed a few scattered chesnut trees and entered the grove where is concealed our sphinx. M. rushed to it with a merry laugh, declaring she would push the monster from the seat he had kept longer than was right. Her gay, fairy-like figure pressed against the rude, grey mass with such mimic might, reminded me of a task assigned, in some elfin tale, to a rebellious hand-maiden of Queen Mab.

We had a little intellectual amusement in deciphering the names of innumerable Julias and Carolines, Rosalinds, Janes, and "Roxany Augustys," inscribed by affectionate jack-knives, upon the bark of the surrounding trees. Some classic gentleman, dolefully destitute of a doxy, had inscribed among them the words, "MEMNON," and "PEUCINIA." I have since heard the story of the merry hour when "Memnon" was inscribed, by a hand which has written many a witty and clever volume. Indeed, indeed there must have been a deal of witchery in the cunning priestess who made that stern old rock breathe such mysterious and enchanting music. I wonder if ever there was anything in that broken champagne bottle which lay at the foot of the rock.

When we had clambered with a world of pains on to the top of the rock, we, too, had music — merry and sad — "music at the twilight hour." Then, as the evening shades deepened in the wood, came low spoken words of memory and of longing for those far away. Alas! if all whom we invoked had come, the grave and the sea must have given up its dead.

With voices softened and mellowed by deeper feeling, my companions sang an "Ave Maria," and we bid farewell, not gaily, to a scene mysteriously consecrated by memories not its own. So, often, in scenes and hours when we invoke the ministers of joy, other spirits arise in their places, and we do not bid them down.

NOTE. In the town of New Marlboro', about twenty miles south of Pittsfield, is one of those curious freaks of nature, a true rocking stone — which the "rolling rock" is not. It is a stone weighing several tons, so balanced upon another that while the slightest touch causes it to oscillate, the greatest force which can be applied, short of lifting its entire weight, will not remove it from its pivot. Similar stones found in the Scottish highlands, have provoked much fierce discussion among the *Savans*. The naturalists claiming them for their kingdom, as a work of Nature, and the antiquarians as stoutly maintaining that they were remains of ancient druidical art. I believe the contest is still feebly maintained, although the discovery of similar rocks in Siberia and America might be supposed to put it at rest. There can be no doubt that the Druids used them like other marvels of nature, to work upon the superstition of their dupes, and it is not unlikely the same may be true of the Indian conjurers.

In this same town of New Marlboro' is a lakelet called the Hermit's Pond, from a certain recluse who took up his residence by its side, some six years before the breaking out of the war of the Revolution, and there lived until the year 1813, when worn out with infirmity and old age — alone and unattended—he died as he had lived; for he forbade any to remain with him even for a single night. The village gossips thought they found a solution of the mystery of his life, in his inveterate hatred of women, and his continually repeated remark of them, "They say they will and they wont."

The good clergyman, who tells this anecdote, adds: "Let none smile at the story of Timothy Leonard;" but for the life of me I can't help it, even though he be "not the only one who has suffered disappointed hope and mortified pride to blot out the social affections and produce wretchedness, misery and ruin." There is something particularly funny in the idea of a man so thoroughly unsophisticated as to think it strange that women should "say they will when they wont." Why, therein lies the very essence of female liberty.

CHAPTER V.

LEBANON SPRINGS.—A DASH AT LIFE THERE.

DOWN in the hilly valley beyond the mountains is Lebanon—New Lebanon—the capital of the Shakers; the seat of the Mineral Springs; the most delightful of watering places; and our Gretna Green. All the world knows Lebanon, but how much of it, about as accurately as the gentleman who, upon the morning after his arrival desired to be shown "the cedars, for which he had been told the place was famous!"

This watering place is a very Mecca for Summer pilgrims, who, soon as Greylock takes off his Winter cap, flock to it in crowds,—some with the quiet matter-of-course air of annual visitors; others, catching a feverish impulse from the city miasma, and rushing away like mad, to flirt with Nature and Hygeia, at the Springs.

It were a curious study to enquire what brings each individual here; but, unfortunately for psychological science, the sojourners at fashionable hotels are neither so communicative nor so docile as the amiable occupants of our public prisons, who never refuse to answer the questions of statistical temperance agents, and nine times out of ten give the very reply which is expected of them. But, lamentable as is this habit of secretiveness, which our fashionables absurdly cherish, we have a ready resource in that supreme faculty for guessing, which makes us Yankees, from Emerson to Andrew Jackson Davis, the incomparable philosophers of the Universe.

It is a pleasant and profitable recreation to exercise this precious faculty of a lazy Summer afternoon on the long verandahs of Columbia Hall. Laziness is the mother of Philosophy. There are some hundreds of human beings scattered about the huge hotel; most of whom may be supposed to have had some motive in coming here, and to have some notion, more or less definite, of the nature of the place and the part they are to play in it. Perhaps, however, we may get as near to what that notion really is, by a tolerably shrewd guess, as by persónal enquiry, — which latter mode of proceeding might also be deemed impertinent; secretiveness being the soul of civilized life. Let us guess, then.

It is easy enough to understand that the student-looking young man, with an orange colored face and sea green spectacles, thinks he has got into an enormous hospital, or perhaps only a mammoth apothecary's shop. He deems those gorgeous, flaunting dames, of whose bright presence he is rather vaguely conscious, of no more real value — since they will not nurse his invalidship — than the colored waters in the apothecary's window opposite.

Those gay ladies themselves, of course, view the matter in a very reverse light. Take one of them, for example — that flirting, chatting, jewelled thing, Madame, the wife of the Wall Street millionaire. With both those clear orbed eyes wide open, she can see little in this magnificent panorama of hill and valley, and in this its life-throbbing heart, more than a splendid ball-room, or gorgeous saloon, — as indeed, for that matter, she would like the wide, wide world to be, — and is vastly annoyed that misery, with her discordant shrieks and disgusting deformities, should presume to spoil the music and mar the decorations.

Look again. You would call yonder a frank, free hearted, undesigning girl. Hear with what joyous, summerly forgetfulness she throws off those snatches of unstudied song; and see how ingenuously the blush rises in her cheek, now she remembers that she is not alone. You would not dream now — would you? — that she looks upon this fair spot only as a mart in which she is to dispose of that dear little commodity — herself — to the best possible advantage? Yet I'll wager you a small farm I have in the clouds, that every note of that outgushing melody was aimed, point blank, at the handsome gentleman who has been conversing, this two hours past, with the pale girl in black. I only hope the minstrel will not be malicious enough to say, the pale girl is "setting her cap" for the handsome gentleman.

Why do n't she turn her thought to drive away the cloud which has settled in the eye of the gloomy-browed man who is pacing the verandah so heavily? Bless us! the Summer sunshine glances off from him, and leaves not a trace of light; he has never sold *his* shadow to Satan. Yet I misdoubt; and so we go on, doubting and misdoubting, guessing and misguessing, sure enough — if we would consider it — of two things; that we shall always hit wide enough of the mark, and never too near the charitable side of it. "Wise judges are we, of each other's actions!"

This Lebanon is not without its vein of romance. How could it be, when youth and age, folly and wisdom, joy and sorrow, love and hatred, life and death, make it their yearly rendezvous? How strange a rendezvous, oft-times! Of those who seek here new thought, new hope, new feelings, how many find only what they bring — a jaded mind and a palsied heart? Mind cramped to the puny pursuit of puny things will not always, upon the mountains, expand and glow with the widening horizon and the purer sunlight. Passion, born luxuriously in the crowded city, grows and strengthens, and will not die in the bracing upland air. Yet is there forgetfulness of lighter woes and less corroding cares, in the gay saloons and woodland drives, as well as marvellous virtue for the diseased body in the bubbling waters and fresh breezes? Care-worn men and women worn with ennui, do get new elasticity of thought and frame; but in what do they seek a balm for the wounded spirit, who bring hither the broken hearted also, — like thee, fair and gentle L., — or was it that thy pure spirit might wing its way to Heaven through purer skies than overhang thy native city?

I said Lebanon had its vein of romance. A bachelor friend of mine, who has been a lounger at Columbia Hall every Summer these ten years past, has a rich fund of stories — humorous, melo-dramatic, and tragical — about those who have fluttered, flattered, flirted, and flitted here in that time. With him, half the Demoiselles who have "made their market" under his eye, are heroines of a quality which would surprise themselves not a little to know, and their husbands a good deal more. It is often a matter of discussion with us, whether, among other connubial revelations, the arts and devices whereby he was entrapped are usually disclosed to the husband. In the absence of data from which to conclude, we always end in the same mists in which we set out. One of my bachelor friend's stories I will venture to repeat, although I perceive it loses half its flavor, for lack of the gusto with which he would dwell upon it.

She would be a Gentleman's Wife.

"More beauty than ever at L. this year," I remarked to my friend, as we sat together one evening, about a year since; it was a common observation, and I thought myself particularly safe in repeating it.

"Hey! what 's that you say?" he ejaculated, after a pause, in which it seemed my words had been following him far down into the depths of reverie. "More beauty than ever at L.! Let me tell you, my dear fellow, that you know nothing at all of the matter. It 's one of the stupid common-places of stupid common people." I bowed to the compliment, and the bachelor went on with a half sigh, "Ah! you should have known us in the reign of the bitter and beautiful Lizzie B., or in that of the wonder-working Mrs. M."

Here the bachelor again relapsed into reverie, and I had time to remark to myself that this hankering after faded flowers, when the world was full of fresh, was an ugly symptom that my friend's own hey-day of beaudom must be on the wane. When people begin to complain

4*

that they can find no beauty, now-a-days, like that which they used to meet, look if they do n't wear wigs, and other falsities of decoration.

"But the most charming season," resumed the bachelor, emerging again into the present, "was that of 184–, when Kate L. was in the ascendant. She was far enough from beautiful, was Mrs. L., but such a winsome way she had with her that we all, to a man, acknowledged her sceptre, — and the most dazzling belle in her realm was ready to die with envy; envy, by the bye, was a vice Mrs. L. was especially free from. Never was woman more ready to recognise and exhibit the charms of her rivals. She surrounded her throne with a constellation of lovely women from far and near, and would let none be eclipsed. A kind-hearted creature was she, and a sensible to boot; a tithe part the jealousy we endured from the splendid Lizzie B. would have made Kate look as ugly as a Bornese ape.

"But it was of her throne maidens that I was going to boast. I wish you could have looked in upon one of our gala nights; we have none such now — (that, *entre nous*, was a fib of the bachelor's). There was a floral ball we had one night in July, — I have some reason to remember it, but no matter, — Mrs. L. had made more than usual exertions in getting up this festival, which was the opening one of the season. The arrangements were perfect; — the floral decorations unique and profuse; the music superb; and the supper just what it should be. But our Lady Patroness was too true a genius to give to these concomitants the monopoly of her attention. With a magic little crow quill by way of wand, she summoned from all manner of retreats the most brilliant assemblage of fair women and distinguished men that I have ever beheld; and when Mrs. L. summoned youth and beauty, you might be sure there was something to be done. I am going to leave them to do it, while I tell you of my cousin Ellen, the fairest of them all.

"You remember Nell — my uncle Fred's Nell — the merriest girl that ever hid deep design under careless laugh. Uncle Fred., you must know, left her an orphan, at twenty, — with exquisite accomplishments, unrivalled tact, and four thousand dollars, with which to make her way in the world, as she best might. Her guardian — a staid, business-like old gentleman, guardian to half the heiresses in the county, as well — when her year of mourning was over, advised her to buy a share in a boarding-school, and earn her living by teaching. 'With your accomplishments and talents, my dear,' — the good, fatherly old man was going on, when he was astonished to find his pretty ward cutting short his speech with —

"'With my accomplishments and talents, my dear guardian, I do n't intend to squeeze my brain like a lemon, to give flavor to some insipid school girl, while I might as well be rivalling her mamma. No! I'll invest in — a husband!' — and here her little foot came down with a will.

"The guardian stared; but he was too sensible a man to oppose a woman whose will was up; and so, under the nominal chaperonship of his wife, Ellen opened her first campaign at Lebanon.

"That night of the floral fête, she stood in the centre

of an admiring group, — a slight, aerial figure, but full of elastic life and vigor; her face transparent with changing light, and her eye overflowing with a flood of love and laughter. She was dressed with wonderful artistic skill; for the life of me I could not imagine how she contrived to arrange her mist-like drapery so that she seemed always on the point of rising into air. I have since heard that it is no mystery among mantua-makers. Among the crowd of women, laden and over-laden with all kinds of flowers, native and exotic, Nell had only twisted in her hair a few snowy, star-shaped blossoms, — the spoil of a mountain excursion. Not a fold of her robes, not a tress on her head but seemed too spiritual for mortal touch. I have since learned that the artistes call this style of dress, *á la Gabrielle.* It is a triumph of genius; but I would not advise any lady weighing over two hundred to try it.

"Frank Leigh was conversing with my etherial cousin in a composed tone, and with a gaze of mere earthly admiration which I could not then have assumed for the world, although Nell and I had been playmates from infancy. I almost shuddered — so strangely had the fancy possessed me — when Frank took her hand, to lead her to the piano, lest she should indeed prove a spirit, and dissolve into thin air.

"'Ellen should be a gentleman's wife,' said a pretty and brilliant widow, by my side.

"Wife! so she was human. 'A gentleman's wife,' I repeated aloud, 'and pray what is a gentleman? — and why should Ellen, more than another, be a gentleman's wife?'

"'Why,' replied the widow, laughing, 'a gentleman,

in Ellen's vocabulary, is a man of elegant manners, with at least one hundred thousand dollars, and a disposition to spend his income in graceful and fashionable follies. Ellen's expensive tastes demand such a husband — and I hope she may get him.'

"'Oh, now I am enlightened,' I said.

"'I am glad to hear it,' rejoined the widow, merrily. But, come with me out into the balcony, and I'll let you into a secret or two.'

"Of course, such an offer was not to be resisted; and before we returned, I was put in possession of much recherché gossip, known only to the initiated.

"There had come that year to the Springs, a fine looking young man, — generous, spirited, of captivating address, and great reputed wealth — Frank Leigh by name; the same who was in attendance upon my cousin Ellen at the floral fête. Of course such a God-send was not to be neglected by anxious mothers, and daughters no less anxious. Mrs. L., finding him clever, fond of sport, and prompt to forward all her gay schemes, had taken him up at once, and installed him her prime minister. Ellen, I need not say, was quite as ready to acknowledge his merits.

"Frank was universally declared to be a 'sweet man,' in the ball-room and drawing-room; but he was not a bit of a dandy; there was nothing of the exclusively ladies' man about him, nothing effeminate in his habits. On the contrary, his tastes were eminently manly. He had yachted on the Atlantic coast, hunted moose in a Maine Winter, and even taken a run after buffaloes into the Sioux country. Here, among the quiet hills, his exuberant spirits found vent in a passion for wild horsemanship. Jehu was a child to him, with the whip; he was sure always to choose some unmanageable foal of gunpowder, that nobody else would come within a rod of; men, even of strong nerves, were of opinion that safer pleasures existed than a seat beside Frank Leigh, on one of his break-neck drives; and as for the women, not a soul of the dear creatures, who would have given their eyes to secure him for a partner at the last night's ball, could be persuaded to trust their ivory necks with him and his 'Lightning' next morning.

"To all this was one most remarkable exception — my brave cousin Nell, who had come out all at once a perfect Di. Vernon. Ah! but it was an inspiriting sight, to see her mounted on her brown steed, leading her panting admirers an aimless race over fields, brakes, briers, and fences, till half the chase forswore all pursuit of her, thereafter.

"But Nelly's favorite seat was in Frank's light buggy, of which she enjoyed undisputed possession — her rivals thinking it a particularly 'bad eminence.' Of course she was the constant companion of our Jehu, and a fit one, as it looked. Travellers marvelled enviously, as Frank's chariot dashed by them, to hear Nelly's clear, ringing laugh, or rattling song; or even at times to see her slight figure braced back, her loose curls flying, and her little hands holding fast the 'lines,' while she urged the foaming horses to yet more impossible speed; —

'Like a dream doth it seem,
When I think of the past;
Up the road gallantly dashing along,
Driving two noble steeds, square built and strong;

Firmly her little hands grasping the reins,
Held them as firmly as lovers in chains.'

"I think the echoes of her merry voice must linger yet among the old woods which skirt the Hancock road. Sure I am that the dwellers in the road-side farm houses yet remember Frank Leigh's dashing equipage, and the gay couple with whom it used to fly by their doors, at such flashing speed.

"Beside his equestrian fancies Frank was exceedingly prone to romantic excursions, and by the aid of the good natured Mrs. L., who was nothing loath, led us upon a hundred wild adventures among the hills, to the great detriment of patent leather and superfine broadcloth. Here, too, Nell was the co-leader with the rattle-brain heir; never a ramble ended until she had joined him in some mad-cap feat or another.

"All this you may be sure gave ample room and verge enough for bitter tongues; but the sage conclusion of one shrewd lady, that, 'some folks could do what other folks could n't,' soon came to be in substance the universal sentiment. Indeed, with all Nelly's faults and follies, it was impossible, when you knew her, to think her capable of anything very wrong.

"One opinion, at least, every body held, and that was, that she was just the girl to charm Frank Leigh — and that she had charmed him to some purpose. Every body but my friend the widow, who, while she admitted the boldness and vigor of Ellen's attack, had a doubt or two as to its success. 'Ellen,' said the widow, 'has a splendid genius for business, but very little experience. Do you not notice that Frank of late, has another companion sometimes on his rides?'

"'What! the timid and femininly delicate Miss P.?'

"'The same; — and with what tender care he curbs his speed when she is his companion?'

"'It is very kind and considerate of him; the jolts and racing in which Ellen delights, would be the death of Miss P. I am sure it is good in him.'

"'Oh, very! And yet is it not possible that she who tames the steed may tame the master?'

"I admitted the noteworthiness of the fact, but trusted to the genius and address of my fair kinswoman for a successful issue of her Summer campaign. Indeed, as the season waned, her star seemed to rise yet higher into the ascendant, while she relaxed no whit of her zeal, but cut madder freaks, rode more daringly, was more than ever the constant companion of Frank, who, although he daily took a quiet drive with Miss P., seemed more than ever devoted to her dashing rival. Everybody said Frank had proposed, was about to propose, or at least was in honor bound to propose to my cousin. He was set down as certain of the fair hands which so gracefully reined in his fiery coursers. Only the widow shook her curls and Miss P. said nothing.

"One bright morning in September, just before the close of the season, Ellen was sitting in the drawing room, surrounded as usual by a group of loungers, — among whom were Mr. Vinton, a gentleman of singularly reserved and quiet manners, and said to be very timid, — and a Miss Phœbe N., a young lady who, in spite of nose and eyes equally awry with her temper, was supposed to be about to seize the quiet gentleman, *vi et armis.*

"'So Frank Leigh has taken us all by surprise, and married,' said some one, joining the group.

"'Married!' 'No?' 'You do n't mean it.' 'How!' 'When?' 'To whom?' exclaimed a dozen voices at once, — the speakers, of course, fixing their eyes considerately upon Nell, except Miss N., who was enabled to turn only one of hers that way, but answered:

"'Oh, to that stupid Miss P. I saw them depart this morning.'

"'I am sure you would not so speak, if you knew her,' said Ellen, indignantly. 'On the contrary, she is a sweet, sensible, and witty girl.'

"'Rather too quiet for me,' mildly remarked the very quiet Mr. Vinton.

"'I do n't see why you should defend her,' snarled the amiable Phœbe to Ellen. 'She has carried off the prize we all assigned to you.'

"'To me!' exclaimed Ellen with real laughter and well affected surprise; 'I am sure I am much obliged to you all. Frank is a noble fellow; but do you know I should have an unconquerable aversion to being rivalled by dogs and horses? — and of course 'Lightning' and 'Ney' will hold equal sway in Frank's heart with his wife.'

"'But we,' began Miss N., with a malicious look —

"'But me no buts!' exclaimed Ellen, interrupting her; 'I would sooner marry a cobbler than a horse-jockey, be he never so rich!'

"Mr. Vinton looked radiantly happy; Miss Phœbe darkeningly the reverse, for it was her 'one woe of life' that her father had began his ascent to wealth in the respectable calling of a cobbler. Ellen saw where her shot hit, and then cast a penetrating glance at Vinton, in whose face she read more than she had suspected."

Here the bachelor paused for breath. "And so," said I, "Miss Ellen lost her Summer's work."

"Not at all," he replied resuming; "you shall hear. Frank Leigh did not choose to fall in love with a woman who rivalled him in the accomplishments of which he was most proud. Even so sensible a fellow as he had a spice of human vanity,— quite enough to cause him to prefer Miss P., who admired his daring feats, to Nelly, who demanded that he should admire hers, and showed, moreover, to all the world that they were not beyond the attainment of a very slight-framed woman. Besides, he could too readily understand all that Nell felt, said, and did; it is not the near view which charms.

"Poor Vinton, however, looking on from a distance, became every day more enamoured; — the qualities which Ellen displayed proved so much the more fascinating from their very strangeness to his own nature. But it is in vain to philosophize about these matters; Vinton, like many a sensible fellow before and since, contrived to get hopelessly into the meshes before he thought of asking how; and the moment he saw the field clear, he resolved to occupy the vacant lovership.

"Our light-hearted Ariadne I suspect was secretly piqued at her desertion; at all events, she gave the new lover a world of encouragement. Indeed, so rapidly did affairs advance, that the same afternoon Mr. Vinton, in a tremor of fear, made a formal proposal, — and was at once accepted. Still more to his joy, Ellen consented—if Miss Phœbe is to be believed, proposed—that the union should take place that same evening; that soon after the demolition of her hopes, Ellen reached their consummation, and was a 'gentleman's wife.'"

"A queer wooing," I said, when the bachelor had concluded. "Was the result happy?"

"Why, the chances were rather against it," he replied; "but fate often treats us better than we would ourselves. The result, I believe, was happy for both."

"And how about the widow and yourself?"

"Is not that the moon rising yonder?" said the bachelor.

CHAPTER VI.*

BERRY POND.

L———, *March* 22, 1852.

MY DEAR S.:—

It is now many months since I promised you an account of a ramble over one of your glorious mountains; and through all these changing moons my promise is unredeemed.

You may have forgotten it,—have at any rate despaired of its fulfilment. And perhaps, if I had remained in P., where the heaven-clad hills stand round about, "as the mountains are round about Jerusalem," in the very presence of their ennobling majesty, I had been too much awed for familiar description, too much delighted for voluble utterance.

But here, with nothing in all the tame horizon but dead sand plains, or faintly swelling hills, still more lifeless in their weak aspiring; here, where nothing, not even the church spires, are so near heaven as the manufactory chimnies,—the awe-inspiring spell of the mountains is broken, while their blue and cloud-like summits, looming over the length of a state in the soft mirage of memory, look lovelier, holier than ever.

* I am indebted for this Chapter to the kindness of a much esteemed and very clever friend.

As a votary, admitted to a costly shrine, stands abashed, and fears to wake the sacred echoes with his unhallowed voice, yet finds in its splendor and its solemn images unfailing themes of story to eager listeners around his humble fire-side, — so I, an exile from the hills I love so well, may exchange my awe struck silence for rapturous speech, and grow garrulous over scenes that once filled me with unutterable pleasure.

It was on a bright, still morning in the painted Autumn, that I started with a friend for Berry Pond. Aye, that 's the name. "I seek no purfled prettiness of phrase," I accept no sickly appellation, borrowed from other scenes, which is thought to sound romantic because unfamiliar, and which was originally noble only because simple and unaffected.

Berry Pond! The name falls sweetly on the ear, and fills the mind with images of cool and crystal waters, and green and sloping shores. It is ringing with the silver ripple of the mountain tarn; it is redolent of wild flowers, and sweet with pulpy fruits.

Berry Pond, however, does not derive its name from the strawberries, the raspberries, the blackberries, and the wintergreen berries, which, by their abundance in its vicinity would justify the appellation; but from an obscure, stout-hearted man, who once dwelt upon its border, and wrung subsistence for a large family of girls out of the margin of its rocky chalice. Honor to him! and let this silver tablet, inscribed with his name, perpetuate his memory as long as English is spoken on the soil he trod!

We pursued our way, in the chill but serene November morning, towards the base of Hancock Mountain, near whose summit lay the object of our journey. Our path was through obscure bye-roads, lined with the dwellings of an industrious and frugal people, standing amid clustering orchards, as if the venerable trees took solemn interest in the drama going on within, and were gathered there to witness it.

My companion was born in one of these abodes, and had passed his life to its high meridian among them; and his memory overflowed with story and incident of merry, or serious, or sad adventure, which these quiet looking homes had seen.

A right pleasant companion, this friend of mine, with his moving memories. An unaffected love of nature, and a quick perception of her beauty and her grandeur, joined to a warm heart and a lively sympathy with all that told of human joy or sorrow, shone unconsciously in his simple language and expressive face. It was almost as well to be with him as to be alone with one's imagination and the spirits of earth and sky; and more cannot be said of mortal friend.

Diverging at last from the highway, we entered through rustic bars upon the private road that winds up the mountain. For a short distance we drove over a level interval, at the mouth of the gorge through which we were to pass; and here we came upon the site of a dwelling, now marked only by the grass-grown cellar, and the mossy and unfruitful trees that seemed to feel alike the loss of human sympathy and human care.

These melancholy mourners around a darkened hearth-stone, creatures of civilization as they were, appeared incapable of receiving the quickening influence of sun and dew direct from the hand of God, like the savage trees that waved their outspread arms above them, and waiting in vain for man's accustomed care, to have pined away in moody sorrow.

Quickly passing this mournful spot, we entered the ravine, down which a brooklet brawled, and began to ascend the mountain by a narrow but excellent road, cut with great labor in the steep hill side. Built to bring down the timber from the summit, it seemed the approach of an indomitable enemy to assault those forest chieftains in their mountain fastness. It is indeed a noble work, and is eloquent of the determination and energy of its builder.

When we began our ascent, the burn was prattling away in familiar accents close at hand. But rising more rapidly than the bed of the channel, the tops of stately trees rooted by the brook-side were soon waving beneath us; and the mingling murmur of the leaves and stream seemed the audible prayer of Nature.

Above us towered the solemn mountain; and the lonely trees which the ruthless axe had spared, subdued and chastened by bereavement, pointed calmly to the sky, and with grave and reverend gesture beckoned us ever upward; while the thoughtless dryads that covered the shorn mountain with a luxurious undergrowth, sported jauntily their gay cashmeres of the latest Autumn style; and with modest shade, and glancing sheen, and merry, tinkling music, invited pause and dalliance.

But upward we ever went, along the steadfast road, till on the one hand the rivulet again appeared close by our side, having climbed the steepest part of the gorge to overtake us, and looking faint and weary with the effort; and on the other the reposing mountain stretched away with gentle and inviting slope, — like the easy ascent of the good man's path, after the steep and toilsome struggle of youth is over.

Leaving our panting horse under a spreading beech, we turned aside from the road, and walked a quarter of a mile to the pond. The undulating ground over which we went, now rugged with coarse ferns and bristling with wild and worthless shrubs, was once a smooth shorn meadow; and all these silent fields, untended and unfenced, once owned a blest allegiance to the arm of toil, and ministered to human happiness. Here rustic maidens spread the new mown grass, and hither rustic wooers came to spend the Summer holiday. Yonder the serried rows of corn-hills, plainly hinted through the faded grass, tell where the last harvest left its stubble, unmolested by the plough. There, where that little mound swells gently from the valley, the sorrowing apple trees point out the spot where dwelt a departed household.

Like the Assyrian king turned into the desolate fields; bearded with hoary moss, and shaggy with unkemped sprays, and gnarled and knotty with dead and decaying boughs, they utter a mournful warning against that rooted grief that seeks refuge in seclusion and "lures us from society where we are safe, to snare us in the solitary desert."

Yet there is something touching in the constancy of these old trees, so unlike the fickle attachments of men. Surely, the apple tree, and not the willow, should be the emblem of enduring sorrow.

Musing thus, we silently moved onwards, till, on

reaching the summit of a ridge, the lakelet burst upon our vision, almost beneath our feet.

To me — a little in advance of my companion — it was not at first comprehended; but, taking the color of my reverie, it seemed another Heaven revealed beneath the sod, as when I looked through tears into an open grave, and saw my Heaven there.

But an exclamation of delight at my elbow, brought out the object of my vision, from the profound into which I had been gazing to the glassy surface, and the heaven beyond the sphere became a crystal lake.

Nothing can exceed the beauty of this pond. Its shores, for a narrow interval, slope gently towards it, and then fall steeply away like the sides of a moulded urn. Its margin is sometimes a beach of silvery sand strewn with blocks of snowy quartz, and delicate, fibrous looking mica; again grassy and green, even now, to the water's edge; and yet again fringed with long eyelashes of birch and hazle trees, that dreamily gaze at their reflection in the mirror.

Its waters are clear and cool, and pleasant to the taste; and with the breathing sky, robed in the candid surplice of the clouds, bending in solemn benediction over it, it seemed the sacramental chalice of nature, and its crystal water, infused with Heaven's own form and hue, seemed changed by a real transubstantiation into the mystic life-blood of the Universe.

We had no need of language, for all that the scene could tell was whispered to the heart of each; so we strolled apart, and worshipped and enjoyed in silence.

Here was no meddling priest to thrust his speculative creed between me and my love to Heaven, and reclining in oriental mood upon a mossy bank, which, thick-spread with fragrant wintergreen, served at once as couch and table, and incense altar, I lifted my heart to God for absolution and blessing, and communed unforbidden.

Oh! not altogether unprofitable these secret musings in the cloisters of the great cathedral. By them we learn to feel that God liveth not alone in history and tradition, but in Nature also, and the world; that He speaketh not alone in the Sinaï-tones of his inspiration, but audibly, too, in the voices of his winds and woods; that, indeed, "He is not the God of the dead, but of the living."

The long, chill shadows of the low trees creeping over me, admonished me to rise, and walking on until I had made the circuit of the pond, I joined my friend who had preceded me, and after pausing awhile to look at the cloud-like blue of the distant Kaatskills, the burly strength of the nearer Taghconic, and the wide panorama of hill and vale that spread between, all robed with the richest colors of the iris, and bathed in the rich, palpable light of the Indian Summer, that filled the valleys to the mountain tops with molten topaz, we turned us from the glory ere yet it had declined, and homeward wound our thoughtful way.

The sun had set when we reached the village, and the threadbare earth stood shivering in the cold and dark, like an aged gentleman suddenly reduced from affluence to want. But from my friend's door, as I paused a moment to see him enter, there came a burst of mingled light and warmth, like the sortie of a garrison to cover the entrance of a friend, and beat back the beleaguring forces of the night.

O ye to whom the blessèd haven of home opens wide its friendly gates to shelter you from the Autumn and the night, thank God the giver for all his blessings, but chiefly for this; and for the rest of us, patience, patience and courage! There shall be a haven for us also.

Yours, Truly,

H.

CHAPTER VII.

THE WIZARD'S GLEN.

A FOUR miles' drive from our village brings the excursionist to a deep gorge, now called the "Gulf," but known in the earlier and less sceptical days of the settlement as the "Wizard's Glen." It is the wildest scene in our immediate neighborhood. A narrow valley is enclosed by steep hills, covered far up their sides with the huge rectangular flint rocks which mark this whole mountain range. You see them scattered every where, from Greylock to Taghconic; but nowhere else — unless, perhaps, at Icy Glen — piled up in such magnificent and chaotic profusion. It is as though an angry Jove had here thrown down some impious wall of the Heaven-defying Titans. Block lies heaped upon block, squared and bevelled, as if by more than mortal art, for of such adamantine hardness are they, that never hand nor implement of man could carve them into symmetry.

In their desolation they seemed charmed to everlasting changelessness; storm and sunshine leave few traces upon them; the trickling stream wears no channel in their obdurate surface; only a falling thunderbolt sometimes splinters an uplifted crag, and marks its course by a scar of more livid whiteness. No flower springs from, no creeping plant clings to them for support, save when the rare Herb Robert would fain cheer them with his tiny blossom; or some starveling lichen strives to shroud the livid ghastliness of their hues.

It is a stern featured place; and yet of a warm Summer afternoon, one — no, not one, it is too intensely sombre for that — but a party can pass a merry hour there, in the cool depths of the ravine. There are some books too, written in a spirit akin to the fantastic and demoniac grandeur of the place, which can be read there with a double zest. Perched between the double angles of a cleft boulder, I once keenly enjoyed some scenes in "Faust." "Manfred" would not be out of place there, nor would some parts of "Festus."

But the best is, to mark how the most humanly merry laughter and the gentlest of gentle voices catch a fiendish echo from the rocky hollows. There is diablerie in the very air; the fairest form I ever knew, as it rose from behind one of those enchanted rocks, looked weird as Lilith, the first wife of Adam. Hecate herself could not have emerged from Hades with half the infernal grace and beauty; I am sure the place is bewitched.

Tradition indeed says that, before the decay of the native tribes, — of whom a scanty remnant were found by the white man in the valley of the Housatonic, — this used to be a favorite haunt of the Indian Priests, or Wizards. Here, it was said, they wrought their hellish incantations, and with horrible rites offered up human sacrifices to Ho-bo-mock-o, the Spirit of Evil. One broad, square rock, which chanced to stand alone in the midst of a conveniently clear space, had the

6

credit of being the Devil's altar-stone. Some crimson stains marked its upper surface, upon which the earlier settlers could not look without a shudder. They were believed to come from the blood of frequent victims,— although, now-a-days, a sceptic with no analysis at all would find little difficulty in resolving them into "traces of iron ore." For my part, until the analysis is made, I hold fast to the older and better opinion of those who believed that around this ensanguined shrine a spectral crew of savage wizards nightly rëenacted the revolting orgies of the past.

I met, not long since, an old man of ninety Winters, — perhaps the last believer in their superstitions. He had heard the story of the shadowy sacrifices from an eye-witness, and related it with a credulous simplicity very difficult to gainsay.

Not far from the year 1770, (as he said,) one John Chamberlain, a brave man and a mighty hunter, of Ashuelot; (now Dalton,) at the close of a hard day's chase, overtook and slew a deer, somewhere within the Wizard's Glen. While he was dressing his quarry, a terrific storm of thunder, lightning, and hail arose,— as Chamberlain averred, with supernatural celerity, as such often seem to do among the mountains. A thunder-storm, even in the ordinary course, is not just the thing to be coveted in this place, by the hardiest deer slayer; but come what will, he must make the best of it. Seeking out, therefore, a spot where the rocks were piled one upon another, with cavernous recesses that formed a sort of natural caravansary beneath, he drew his deer under one boulder and ensconced himself snugly under the shelter of another.

Thus protected, he betook himself to such slumbers as he might get, which turned out to be not the most peaceful. The thunder crashed, the lightning glared and the wind howled in a manner which seemed to our poor John altogether demoniacal. Sleep, in such a hurly-burly of the elements, was out of the question; so, raising himself up he looked out among the rocks, as he could very well do by the aid of the scarcely intermittent lightning.

You may be sure that, with all his courage, our hunter was not quite pleased to find himself in full view of the Devil's altar-stone. It was an ugly predicament, to say the least of it; but there was no help in the case, and he had only to make the best he could of this also, which turned out to be bad enough again. His eyes once fixed upon it, the haunted spot kept them riveted by a terrible fascination, while Chamberlain reflected upon his position in a state of mind which was doubtless far enough from that of philosophic calmness.

Very soon, however, his reflections were interrupted by a wilder rush of the storm, and a yet broader and more vivid flash of lightning, which illumined the whole valley and revealed the horned Devil himself, seated upon a broken crag and clothed in all the recognised paraphernalia of his royalty. Chamberlain thought him a very Indiany-looking devil indeed, which rather pleased him afterwards to tell, for he was no lover of the Indian race.

This was apparently a gala night with Satan, although none of the guests were yet arrived. He was not now going to battle or to work, but rather to hold a royal drawing-room, by way of enjoying himself and receiving homage. His Sable Majesty is well aware that they who would maintain authority must never too much relax their dignity; so, upon this occasion he sat enthroned with a very commanding and royal grace, while the arrowy lightnings shot in circles round his head, — very much, I judge, as you may have seen the swallows dart and soar of a Summer evening, around an old church steeple.

His Majesty had not long to wait for his loving lieges, for suddenly from the darkness a huge, gaunt-framed wizard leaped out and mounted the altar-stone. If Chamberlain has not painted him blacker than he deserves, this High Priest of Satan was a most villainous-looking rascal. His raw-boned and ghastly visage was painted in most blood-thirsty ugliness; scalps, dripping with fresh blood, hung around his body in festoons; on his own scull, by way of scalp lock, burned a lambent blue flame; his distended veins shone through the bright copper-colored skin as if they were filled with molten fire for blood — and, as for his eyes, they glowed with a fiercer light than those of the arch fiend himself; from whence Chamberlain maintained that an Indian Priest was at least one degree more devilish than the Devil himself.

The present was evidently a very potent magician, for at his call a throng of ghastly and horrible phantoms came pouring in from every nook and cranny of the valley — each with a shadowy tomahawk and a torch, which did not burn with the honest and ruddy glare of pitch pine, but with a blue color and sulphurous odor, that revealed unmistakeably at what fire they had been lighted.

Every ghost, as he came in, made a profound obeisance to the rock throned Satan, and then took his place in the circle around the altar-stone. By and bye, the Chief Priest set up a wild, howling chant, and away went the whole rabble rout, yelling and rushing round the altar in a mad, galloping sort of a dance, in which they lifted their feet all the while, as if treading upon burning coals or red-hot iron — a step which is only learned in the dancing-schools down below. Many more such diabolical antics they cut, which, as they would neither be profitable by way of example or warning, it does not matter to tell.

At last they paused, and Chamberlain thought it about time for them to take themselves off; but they were far enough from that. On the contrary, two barbarous looking phantoms — who might in life have been familiars to a savage inquisition — presented themselves, leading between them a beautiful Indian maiden, robed only in her own long, black hair. At another moment the beholder might have admired her graceful proportions and regular features, — as he did when he afterwards remembered them, — but now his senses were too much absorbed by horror. Not a word the poor girl spoke, but, stupified and silent, looked round from one unrelenting face to another, as if at a loss to comprehend what it all meant. Poor girl! she soon knew; for one of the familiars, seizing her rudely around the waist, placed her upon the altar-stone, before the priest. Then she shrieked — so wildly that the hunter declared the echo never ceased ringing in his ears to his dying day; — what part she had to perform then was no longer doubtful. But she shrieked not again nor spoke,

— only looked up into the fiery eyes of the priest so piteously that it seemed his heart should have melted, had it been formed even of flint like the stone on which he stood; but it had been hardened in more infernal fires.

So he took up his demoniac howl again, and went capering madly around the maiden. Then, suddenly pausing before her, he raised his hatchet and the whole phantom circle gathered closer around him, as if to gloat more nearly over their victim's pangs. It seemed the sacrifice was about to be consummated; but as the weapon was raised, the maiden's eyes (averted from it) met those of Chamberlain. The kind-hearted hunter, in whom compassion had overcome fear, could no longer restrain himself; so, taking out his Bible, he pronounced the great NAME, — and with a terrific crash of the elements the whole scene vanished, leaving him in impenetrable darkness, — for although the lightnings ceased, as if they had accompanied their master in his flight, yet the rain fell faster than ever.

When the morning came, Chamberlain would have taken it all for a dream, for, exhausted with fatigue and excitement, he had fallen into a deep sleep; but he found that the wizards, unable to harm him, while protected by the holy volume, had revenged themselves by stealing his deer, and perhaps giving it to their familiars, the bears — for there were bears in those days — so that there can be no manner of doubt as to the truth and accuracy of Chamberlain's story.

There is many another legend of this haunted dell; as for this, I hope you place the same implicit confidence in it which my old informant did.

Passing through the gorge very late, one piercing cold Winter night, the place looked very weird to me. The frozen air was still as death; the white moonlight was reflected from the snow, as I fancied, with more of pallor than of brightness, and I heard a shriek which I tried to believe came from the maiden victim. But it may have been the scream of some far-off locomotive. Confound those "resonant steam eagles!" — there's never a shriek, from Cape Cod to the Taghconics — though with the ghostliest ring to it — but they get the credit.

CHAPTER VIII.

OUR RURAL CEMETERY.

An eye, observant of such things, finds few studies more delicately curious than to watch those customs which are rapidly, but almost imperceptibly, clustering to form our national character. The rude and chaotic elements seem, even while we look upon them, to become conscious of order's laws, and to crystalize around the nucleus of puritanic vigor into the shapely and lustrous gem. Among these customs, not the least purely beautiful is that of the consecration of rural cemeteries in peaceful and retired spots, — where the dead may find undisturbed repose, and the living may weep over them, far removed from the noisy clang of jarring throngs. There Nature and Art combine to dissociate from Death his long accustomed horrors; and there, though he still reign King of Terrors, he is content to wear, not his iron crown, but his chaplet of the poplar leaf — dark indeed without, but silver white within.

Are not our American morals of the grave — where they have developed themselves in their highest perfection — beautiful and peculiar? Think how many of the purest elements from other times and other nations have combined to form them! The Egyptian's sacred reverence for the ruined palace of the soul; the Grecian's graceful celebration in song and sculpture; the Frenchman's clinging, passionate love for the perishing body; and overruling and pervading all, our fathers' stern but hopeful faith that the immortal soul stays not nor lingers, on its way from Earth, in any retreat—however lovely and however consecrated. After all, it is for the living, and not the dead, that we set apart our holy grounds.

Such were some of the thoughts which passed over me, as I went out to-day to witness the consecration of our Rural Cemetery. Nor could I refrain from some sad reminiscences of one soft and balmy day, many years ago, when, with a party of youthful friends I went out to unite with the people of my far off native city, in ceremonies like those which I to-day have witnessed among strangers. It was one of those occasions to which we look back as to a "far off isle in the stormy sea of years;" one of those land-marks by which we determine how far we have advanced towards the farther shore.

More than half the little group who were with me that Summer day, have fallen in their youth, and are laid to sleep among the dim woods of that oak crowned hill, which we then dedicated to peace and consecrated by the sweetly significant name of "Mount Hope." Upon how many of those who remain does a painful sense of loneliness weigh, until they almost wish that they too had their home in its bosom.

As to-day I looked among the crowd who had collected at the new cemetery, the countenance of a fair girl, known to me only by name, recalled, as it had often done before, the memory of another grandly solemn burial place, on the distant plains of Pegepscot, surrounded by dark and lofty woods, —

> "Where the solemn night wind marches
> Through the pine's cathedral arches
> Solemnly."

It was there that one bearing the same name, and in whose veins flowed the same blood, was long ago laid in youth to rest. Around her tomb rise the monuments of divines, and scholars, and statesmen; and the more touching memorials of vanished youth and beauty cluster near; but none have such a fascination for the lingerer as the white tablet on which is inscribed the name and age of the President's daughter. How often will he lean over that sepulchral marble and strive to depict to his fancy the manner and fashion of the beautiful who sleeps so unconsciously below.

The solemn ceremonies of to-day, thus half sadly, half pleasantly recalled other days in those distant cemeteries. In the clear sunshine of October, we assembled by thousands, — young men and maidens, old men and children, — on a grove shaded knoll, surrounded by lawns and lake, wood and stream, to be hereafter more emphatically than others —

> "the solemn decorations all
> Of the great tomb of man."

We had come in sadness, although not in sorrow. Nothing impaired the becoming solemnity of the scene; and when the full swell of the chorals had ceased, when the sacred words of Scripture were read and the consecrating prayer was said, all shared the emotions of the orator as he began: "Have we been persuaded — an assembly of the living — to look upon the very ground where we may sleep? Impelled by a desire to do honor to the dead, have we come within the precincts of a spot where every shadow seems now to deepen, and where the mountains point so significantly to the skies?"

Few things of the kind are so classically and christianly beautiful as was this entire Address, by Rev. Mr. NEILL, of Lenox — one of our finest scholars and most eloquent divines.

Then followed the Poem, by OLIVER WENDELL HOLMES, — of which I cannot resist the temptation to copy a great part. None can feel an adequate admiration for the poetry of Dr. Holmes, unless they hear it from his own lips. But read: —

"Angel of Death! Extend thy silent reign!
Stretch thy dark sceptre o'er this new domain!
No sable car along the winding road
Has borne to earth its unresisting load;
No sudden mound has risen yet to show
Where the pale slumberer folds his arms below;
No marble gleams to bid his memory live
In the brief lines that hurrying Time can give;
Yet, O Destroyer! From thy shrouded throne
Look on our gift; this realm is all thine own!

"Fair is the scene; its sweetness oft beguiled
From their dim paths the children of the wild;
The dark-haired maiden loved its grassy dells,
The feathered warrior claimed its wooded swells,
Still on its slopes the ploughman's ridges show
The pointed flints that left his fatal bow,
Chipped with rough art and slow barbarian toil, —
Last of his wrecks that strews the alien soil!

"Here spread the fields that waved their ripened store
Till the brown arms of Labor held no more;

The scythe's broad meadow with its dusky blush;
The sickle's harvest with its velvet flush;
The green-haired maize, her silken tresses laid,
In soft luxuriance, on her harsh brocade;
The gourd that swells beneath her tossing plume;
The coarser wheat that rolls in lakes of bloom,—
Its coral stems and milk-white flowers alive
With the wide murmurs of the scattered hive;
The glossy apple with the pencilled streak
Of morning painted on its southern cheek;
The pear's long necklace strung with golden drops,
Arched, like the banyan, o'er its hasty props;
The humble roots that paid the laborer's care
With the cheap luxuries wealth consents to spare;
The healing herbs whose virtues could not save
The hand that reared them from the neighboring grave.

"Yet all its varied charms, forever free
From task and tribute, Labor yields to thee;
No more when April sheds her fitful rain
The sower's hand shall cast its flying grain;
No more when Autumn strews the flaming leaves
The reaper's band shall gird its yellow sheaves;
For thee alike the circling seasons flow
Till the first blossoms heave the latest snow.
In the stiff clod below the whirling drifts,
In the loose soil the springing herbage lifts,
In the hot dust beneath the parching weeds
Life's wilting flower shall drop its shrivelled seeds;
Its germ entranced in thy unbreathing sleep
Till what thou sowest mightier angels reap!

"Spirit of Beauty! Let thy graces blend
With loveliest Nature all that Art can lend.
Come from the bowers where Summer's life-blood flows
Through the red lips of June's half open rose,
Dressed in bright hues, the loving sunshine's dower;
For tranquil Nature owns no mourning flower.
Come from the forest where the beech's screen
Bars the fierce noonbeam with its flakes of green;
Stay the rude axe that bares the shadowy plains,
Staunch the deep wound that dries the maple's veins.
Come with the stream whose silver-braided rills
Fling their unclasping bracelets from the hills,
Till in one gleam, beneath the forest's wings,
Melts the white glitter of a hundred springs.
Come from the steeps where look majestic forth
From their twin thrones the Giants of the North—
On the huge shapes that crouching at their knees,
Stretch their broad shoulders, rough with shaggy trees.

Through the wide waste of ether, not in vain
Their softened gaze shall reach our distant plain;
There, while the mourner turns his aching eyes
On the blue mounds that print the bluer skies,
Nature shall whisper that the fading view
Of mightiest grief may wear a heavenly hue."

With this let us close our notes of this day of high but melancholy pleasure.

CHAPTER IX.

AN HOUR IN OUR CEMETERY — BEING BRIEF RECORDS OF CONVERSATION.

"I could wish to have the shadow of Death upon me till my soul had truly and rightly felt it."

MOUNTFORD.

ONE stilly Sabbath evening, as the full splendor of the harvest moon was following hard upon the retiring gleams of a cloudless sunset, we found ourselves at the gate of our new cemetery. It was not long since, with admiring thousands, we had there listened to the memorable eloquence and poetry which had consecrated it to Peace; but the crowd had gone their way, and the place was very solitary now in its loveliness. It was as though the Peace which had been invoked descended visibly upon the sacred grove.

"All sounds were hushed — of labor or of mirth."

Only, consonant with the hour and the place, the monotonous tolling of a distant bell, and the low, lulling murmur of the Housatonic soothed the ear and invited us within the leafy sanctuary. We entered.

EDWARD BRANCTON. We have been often here, Godfrey, and yet to-night how novel seems the familiar scene. With what sharpness of pencilling is drawn this net work shadow of bough and leaf; and that single oak by the lakelet's side, how finely it stands out from its dark back-ground!

GODFREY GREYLOCK. Yes; and how perfectly the unruffled water mirrors back its undistorted image! The image is fairer than the substance.

EDWARD. There is deeper gloom, too, under those sombre hemlocks; and see! up yonder knoll, how the ghostly forms of the sheeted birch start out upon us from the wood;—

"Nothing but doth suffer a night change,
Into something rich and strange."

Such a change as our fathers' fancied came over the wight, who, on a weird night like this, strayed into the charmed circle of the fairy folk. Oh, what a fit realm were this for fairy queen! I am not sure that it is not enchanted ground.

GODFREY. Alas, this place shall bear the record of sadder mutations than those of superstitious fancy or of changing lights. They who shall hereafter tread these avenues will find food for more melancholy, perhaps more profitable meditations than ours.

EDWARD. Yet hath the new tomb, wherein was never man laid, its own peculiar lesson. There is a singular charm for me in our graveless cemetery—this virgin bride of Death.

GODFREY. Doubtless it is well for us to be here. We do well to contemplate anything upon which the shadow of Death hath fallen. Whatever that dark spirit touches he invests with a portion of his own sublime terrors; and after the unapproachable ONE, where shall we look for such awful majesty! It is my passion to meditate upon him where the garish light of life maintains no contests with his congenial shades.

EDWARD. I, now, on the contrary, would bid the most cheerful light of day, or such a silver radiance as this, fall upon the tomb I love; I cannot grudge a portion of the common sunshine to paint the daisy that grows above the dead. Your gloomy mould-collecting cypress and yew are not for me. Let us plant about the resting places of our departed the feathery elm, the maple, and the silver-leafed poplar. Divest the tyrant of your imagination of his horror-striking sceptre; he reigns only by your submission.

GODFREY. It is in vain. Christianise or stoicise as we will, the last change — the mysterious soul parting — remains the great terror of our humanity. Why should we wish it otherwise? The soul trembles with awe, as it expands to receive the impression of some overpowering object of sense — the Alps, the ocean, or St. Peter's dome. Should it not thrill at the passage from the little known to the boundless unknown?

EDWARD. And yet, by Faith, martyrs and dying saints have entered upon that mysterious path with smiles and songs of triumph.

GODFREY. And so by their sort of faith have pagans and infidels; but so could not I. Do you think that Columbus smiled, when, in the morning's grey, he beheld, dim and indistinct, the reality of a life's long dream? Neither should you, to behold, in the dim light of Death, the eternal shore, — although you knew it to be the heavenly goal of a life's best hopes. Be assured we make too lightly of this matter when we speak of crowning the majesty of Death with roses. There is mockery in it and treason, that I, for one, will not plot against the King of Terrors.

EDWARD. Yet surely you would not set up a skeleton image for us to worship!

GODFREY. By no means. Why personify Death at all? Let us leave him rather as does Milton — a vast, awful, but undefined image, which the soul may contemplate in varying but ever reverential mood. We wrongly strive to make Death familiar to our thought.

EDWARD. There can be no irreverence or profanation in holding frequent and familiar converse with Death, since HE — only whose stern minister the dark angel is — invites us to commune with Himself as with a friend.

GODFREY. The oft communion is well; the familiar, sentimental talk of Death, I deem to be ill, unreal, meaningless, not to endure when the reality comes; a trick to soothe the terrors of a distant contemplation of Death, which will fail us altogether at the last, in the near dread presence. We presume too much on the communion we are permitted to hold with our Maker. I have heard pious, good men address the Ruler of the Universe in flippant tones, and even with advice — such as they would not dare address to the merest village potentate. Let us think of Him with reverence, as our Creator, our King, our Judge; with greater trembling as our Father and Friend. Let us speak of Him with profoundest awe, as the Most High GOD, — fearful in praises, doing wonders; as did the royal

Psalmist, bowing before him with the devotion of the lowliest subject.

EDWARD. With the affection of a child for a parent as well.

GODFREY. Yes, with that filial affection of the Orientals — more informed with awe than the homage of the most abject slave of the most iron despotism.

EDWARD. Well, let these cheerful groves and glades answer you. This lake, which they have called by the name of "St. John the Beloved;" — this oak, which stands here pointing constantly to Heaven.

GODFREY. This oak. Do you know L. calls it the "Dial Oak?" whose circling shadow, at some time every day, points each man to his grave. By the bye, can you repeat those fine lines of John Malcolm's, on a dial?

EDWARD. In part.

"Upon a dial stone
Behold the shade of time,
Forever circling on and on
In silence more sublime
Than if the thunder of the spheres
Pealed forth its march to mortal ears!

"It meets us hour by hour,
Doles forth our little span,
Reveals a presence and a power
Felt and confessed by man; —
The drops of moments, day by day,
That rocks of ages wear away.

"Woven by a hand unseen,
Upon that stone survey
A robe of dark sepulchral green,
The mantle of decay, —
The fold of chill oblivion's pall,
That falleth with yon shadow's fall!

"Day is the time for toil, —
Night balms the weary breast, —
Stars have their vigils, — seas, awhile,
Will sink to peaceful rest; —
But round and round the shadow creeps
Of that which slumbers not nor sleeps!

"Before the ceaseless shade
That round the world doth sail,
It's towers and temples bow the head,
The pyramids look pale,
The festal halls grow hushed and cold,
The everlasting hills wax old.

"Coeval with the sun,
Its silent course began,
And still its phantom race shall run
Till worlds with age grow wan, —
Till darkness spread her funeral pall,
And one vast shadow circles all!"

Godfrey. See, while you were repeating, the moon has gone down behind Onota, and the shadows are deepening around us. Have they, too, no lesson?

CHAPTER X.

LENOX AND ITS SCENERY.

In tradition, and in books, far and near, is Lenox known as one of the most charming mountain towns in New England. The traveller never forgets the joy which breaks in upon him through his gratified senses, when on a fresh Summer morning, he mounts its hill for the first time. He knows not whether to admire most the rural neatness of its quiet village, the pure, sweet air whose briskness so braces his nerves, or the varied beauty of its landscapes. How it cools a fevered brain, and restores the elasticity of a depressed spirit, to feel oneself treading freely upon green earth unbounded by iron railings, and to gaze into a blue sky unclouded by smoke and dust! Those only who leave the hot terraces and singed air of a city, can worthily panegyrize the dewy mornings, the cool, luxuriant verdure, and the wide prospect which regale the senses in a mountain region like ours. We take an honest pride in watching the glow of health gradually suffusing the pale cheeks of those who come to snuff our air. How buoyant become the spirits, let loose from sickly confinement upon that which "every natural heart enjoys!" How ring the merry shouts up our joyous hills!

The stranger will need no guide to find such charms. He need but confidently open the porches of his senses and it shall go very hard if they fail to stream in through each inlet. It matters not so much at what season he come, so he bring with him a mind capable of appreciating and enjoying a beauty which changes with every varying aspect of the heavens. There is the balm of a May morning; the quickening vitality of the warmth of June; and the mellow glory of October, — as well as the comparative freshness of our July and August, to those who follow the example of the Roman, in fleeing from "mad dogs and streets black with funerals, to gather the first figs of the season in the country." They are doubtless wise in the light of their own philosophy, who seek a rural retreat like ours, for a month or two, — ready to hasten back to the delights of "trivial pomp and city noise," as soon as the dog-star abates his rage a little; but let not such presume to fancy themselves at all conversant with the budding, ripening, and fading beauties of the "swelling year," as it unfolds itself in our hill country!

But to the mere lover of natural scenery, though he linger, never tiring of the varied pleasures revealed to him, the half has not been told. He who regards our village only as a part of the "great world of eye and ear," may be deeply impressed with its claims upon his admiration, and yet go away but ill prepared to do justice to its truest beauties. A Berkshire Winter is almost bleak enough to become a proverb; but some of us, who have braved its blasts, would not barter the prospect which it brings, of the genial delights of warm fire-sides and warm hearts, for the prospect of an

Italian spring, or of three months in the spice-groves of Araby the blest! He who would give Lenox its due meed of praise, must be able to interweave the first impressions of the stranger with the matured acquaintance of the resident. If that cannot be his lot, we would tell him that here is the wealth of personal worth; that here have lived, and still live, many whom the world delight to honor; that here, in a quiet seclusion congenial to thought and fancy, reflecting and gifted minds have plumed many "wingéd words" for a ceaseless flight.

In order to get the best distant view of Lenox, you must approach it by the Lebanon road. As you wind down the mountain, you get occasional glimpses of the spires of a half-hid village, on an eminence east of you. Soon a turn in the road brings you in sight of a broad, cultivated swell of ground, sloping gently up from beneath you, on the brow of which, so embosomed in shrubbery that it promises to reveal much more than you are now permitted to see, stands the main part of the village. The spire which you see upon the left is upon the steeple of the Congregational church, which overlooks the village from an eminence north of it. As you approach, the tufts of trees open partially and disclose a cluster of white houses stretching a third of a mile from north to south, and upon several streets converging towards the centre of the village; the whole so thick set with maples and elms that very few of the buildings can be distinctly seen. While nearing the village from this direction, you have on the right a fine view over a broad, green valley, extending into the towns of Stockbridge and West Stockbridge, and cooped snugly in on all sides by ridges of hills. It was while travelling over this same road, with this lovely scene beneath them, that a party of Hungarians, who had come to Lenox in search of employment, could not refrain from raising their hands and shouting their admiration to the full extent of their English, in repeated exclamations of "beauty! beauty!"

We have entered Lenox by an unusual route. If the cars on the Housatonic railroad set you down at the dépôt, about two miles from the village, you will have a carriage ride all the way up hill. The road for a part of the way is delightful. The murmur of a brook on each side of you is a pleasant exchange for the hoarse mumbling of the cars, and you become sensible of a purer and fresher breeze fanning your cheek as you ascend. The wild luxuriance of the scenery on all sides, the perfect stillness of the air, save when broken in upon by the songs of birds, singing as with no fear of being disturbed in the security of their leafy labyrinths; the whole impression of a scene so wild and native is so utterly dissonant from the ideas suggested by the sound of the whistle, that, — if we may forestall the traveller in his reflections, — the incongruity of the tales told to your senses will be the burden of your thoughts. A railroad through the marts of trade, on the banks of the Hudson, or even over the Rocky Mountains, whither the gold region invites, you could contemplate with quiet complacency; but here, where the golden age still seems to linger, the vulgar snortings of the iron-horse grate harshly upon the ear. If the Latin poet thought that the heart of that man who first thwarted the designs of Heaven in cutting off the land from the "unsociable ocean," by tempting it with his impious bark, must have been girt with "brass and triple steel," judge, O ye gods! how insensate must that wretch have been who first turned the leaden eyes of railway harpies toward our quiet village! How must slumber have forever forsaken his eyelids who thus "murdered sleep!"

But your memory having been recalled to the fact that you are on the way to Lenox, you will be wondering, long before you get a glimpse of it, where there can be a village so far up. Your expectation almost tires of seeing it perched, invitingly, on some hill-top now hid from view, to which the consideration that a "city set on a hill" ought not to be hid, certainly brings no relief; but notwithstanding your reflections, up and still up you go, till you suddenly find yourself in the back streets of the village. Lenox has the highest elevation of any village in the county, being at least thirteen hundred feet above the sea level. Yet situated on a hill among hills, protected somewhat by a sort of amphitheatre of ridges, without being shut away from the cool breezes which sweep so gratefully over these mountain ranges in Summer, the thermometer actually indicates less extremes of heat and cold than in the villages located in the adjacent valleys. Whether it be principally owing to its position, or to that combined with the pleasing inducement to walking and riding offered by the shady avenues and delightful roads diverging in so many directions from Lenox, or to the superadded effect of the cheerful morality which prevails, that the cheeks of the young wear such a peculiarly healthy glow, it is certain that this never fails to attract the notice of strangers. It was with less surprise than gratification, considering the favorableness to health of the locality, and of the pursuits to which its inhabitants are devoted, that on a recent examination of the record of deaths, faithfully kept for the past ten years, we found Lenox to be by far the healthiest town in the county.

The public buildings of the county are situated in Lenox. The Court-House is a brick edifice, of unexceptionable taste in its architecture, and furnished with a library for the use of the bar. Here also is an Academy, which being the oldest in Berkshire, presents a history of success through fifty years, seldom equalled by institutions of its kind. The principal Hotel — so situated as to command a favorable view, both of the village and distant scenery — has become, under the care of its efficient proprietor, M. S. Wilson, Esq., a favorite resort for visitors from the cities.

Unlike the rugged, grotesque scenery to be met with in some parts of Berkshire, the landscapes adjacent to Lenox are rather of a picturesque character. There is hardly a rod of level land in the town, yet there is very little that can be called broken. Even the hills, notwithstanding their bold proximity, present such a social and inviting aspect, that no one in whose ear natural scenery speaks an intelligible language, will remain long in sight of them without accepting their invitation to climb their sunny sides. Bald Summit, in the south-west, tenders as tempting a request as any; he is a brave "specular mount," and will repay you with a prospect in grandeur and beauty not easily surpassed. The view he gives you is wide, rich, and joyous, — nothing in the range of your vision frowns.

If you want a guide-book, take "L'Allegro" with you, and passing from swell to swell, from hill top to hill top, all the region over, you will find nothing to mar the gayety of its pictures. Sunny slopes, covered with "meadows trim;" delightful swells undulating over broad, green valleys; hills on whose sides cultivated fields alternate with luxuriant wood-land patches—the very summits of many crowned with the sweetest pasturage; little lakes of peerless beauty smiling out of their sheltered beds among the hills; villages in several directions, embowered in shrubbery that tempers the glow of their white buildings; the whole scene begirt in the distance, in some directions, by sturdy elevations, and in others by long ridges drawing a clear line against the sky, are the main features of a picture,—for the coloring and details of which you must be indebted to Bald Summit himself.

But as after a general survey of a face you always return to take a second look at the eye, turn now to gaze awhile at the eye of our landscape. It is a blue eye now, and looks out lovingly from underneath sheltering brows; but when Heaven's face scowls over these hills, it blackens and scowls too. It sparkles and glances in the jocund light of morning; we have loved to watch it, growing soft and deep, like a dying man's eye at sunset!

A lady, of whom we intend shortly to speak, has given this little lake the name of the "Stockbridge Bowl." It is the largest of the three lakes near our southern border, and is a gem we take no little pride in showing to the stranger. You must get a view of it from the south-eastern shore, that the dark shade of the elms upon its northern and western sides may throw into higher effect the magnificent sweep of its margin. Go and listen to the music of the ripples on its pebbly beach, when a morning breeze ruffles its surface; go and catch a "noontide dream" from their fainter murmur at mid-day; go and watch the shadows of the mountains darken and lengthen, and melt in its molten crystal. When your ears are wearied with the coarse din of business thoroughfares, and your eyes aching with the glare of brick walls, many will be the times that you will long for another draught of beauty from the Stockbridge Bowl.

It becomes us to observe all circumspection in speaking of the personal characteristics of those among whom our book will doubtless find its way; but we cannot forbear trespassing on the privacy of the people of Lenox sufficient to pay what we deem a just tribute to their mental and moral qualities. Leaving out — as we are always bound to do — the few who tower above, and the few who crouch below the main *mass*, we never knew a people who had, to a greater degree, the rare, happy faculty of holding fast the "golden mean." Elevated by education and refinement far above the rusticity so characteristic of too much of our New-England yeomanry, yet they do not aspire to the pomp of gay life, or the pageantry of fashion. Not anxious for the excitements of intense exertion, as indeed they are remote from the great centres of commercial and political agitation, they will win your admiration more by their intelligence, their fidelity, and their affection, than by the cloud of dust they raise on the arena of the world's strife. While you will find in them an unaffected appreciation and a warm love for the beauties of their hills, and lakes, and skies, each one is inclined to prefer his own fireside to all else; and at their firesides you must meet them, if you would know them as they really are. We have often thought, perhaps not justly, but certainly with great admiration for their philosophy, that if all obstacles to the realization of their ideal of life were removed, it would be one —

> "Whose even thread the Fates spin round and full,
> Out of their choicest and their whitest wool."

CHAPTER XI.*

LENOX AS A JUNGLE FOR LITERARY LIONS.

THE rural beauty of its locality, and the unobtrusive deference universally paid to real worth, by its inhabitants, have attracted within the precincts of Lenox many persons of literary eminence. This fact has long associated its name with that kind of celebrity, which, through an affection for genius itself, is always accorded to its local habitation. No ordinary interest invests the spot where the private life of a distinguished person is passed; and, partly because persons of genius are very generally characterized by eccentricities, and partly because every thing connected with those we love has a peculiar claim upon our regard, there is nothing that we seize with more avidity than details of their *personelle* — their daily walk and conversation — the way in which they demean themselves, when they have laid aside the buskin, or dismounted from the Pegasus of their coursings, and become common men and women — fellow mortals. Grateful as are the tones of their voices, when addressing us as "Gentle Reader," it is with a far more home-felt delight that we hear them,

* For this and the preceding Chapter, I am indebted to the pen of Mr. BUCKHAM, of Lenox.

8*

when companions of their walks, or fellow visitants of their favorite haunts, even in imagination.

In attempting to play the *cicerone* for you, in these trippings, we only wish that while we observe the limits of propriety and courtesy, in making such disclosures, we could bring materials for your entertainment at all commensurate with the distinguished merit of the persons to whom we shall introduce you.

And first, of MISS SEDGWICK. At the bare mention of her name, we seem to see a whole troup of sunny-faced children gathering close around us — for while hers is a name which men of the sturdiest intellects have long associated with whatever is graceful in literature, we know of none more adapted to beguile "young children from play, and the old from the chimney corner." Yet we cannot speak of Miss Sedgwick as we would, for we venture to say that the retirement of her private life would reveal more to admire the more it was unfolded; we cannot even speak freely of the cordiality of her manners, the charms of her conversation, or the winning grace of her whole life; for if we knew aught of these things beyond others, it could only have been from her own confiding courtesy. We are therefore reluctantly compelled to regard her in a position which she shares with many others, and to place the great, in her character, more prominently before the eye than the good.

The first part of Miss Sedgwick's literary career was spent in Stockbridge, the place of her birth. Many of the beautiful descriptions of scenery to be met with throughout her writings, are transcripts of impressions made upon her mind by the scenery among which her youthful imagination was nurtured, in the lovely valley of the Housatonic. There is no trait in her mental constitution which gives more grace to all the goings forth of her life — intellectual and social — than its inborn affinity for natural beauty. She has done much to induce a livelier sympathy with the beautiful in the minds of all, but more especially in the humbler classes, who have been supposed to be almost, of necessity, out of the reach of its refining influence. She has given names, and by her descriptions, attractiveness, to many of the most admired features of Berkshire scenery; and our horticultural exhibitions are always graced by a bouquet of flowers reared by her own hand.

Neither in her intellect nor her feelings has Miss Sedgwick been trammelled by any of the straight-laced notions of a school. The simplicity of nature has never been trained by art to rigidity; nor have the spontaneous promptings of intelligence and good-will been curbed into too decent a conformity with conventional models. Her views on all subjects embracing human relations, are uncommonly liberal and tolerant, and are only equalled in breadth by her universal sympathy with the true and the good, wherever found. If the mode in which she ridiculed the extravagances into which religious doctrines, held sacred by so large a share of her countrymen, had been suffered to run, and which got for the "New-England Tale" the reputation of being a covert attack against the doctrines themselves, seems to form an exception, — we can only say that it must be an exception, for it certainly has no parallel in her writings, and no sanction in her private character. Whilst we must acknowledge that it is a most perilous undertaking to ridicule religious excesses, — and whilst we must in candor say that we think Miss Sedgwick has erred upon the more dangerous side, yet when we take into consideration the fact that the Tale was commenced as a religious tract, with a sincere desire to open men's eyes to matters which may have needed correction, and that, after it had grown into a book under the author's hands, she entertained no idea of publishing it, until almost compelled by her friends, we cannot think that it ought to impair the validity of our assertion, drawn from her later writings, and the impression of her private life, that she has a cordial love for all that is lovely, and a ready sympathy for all that is worthy of it. Though strongly American in her attachments, she could yet see and acknowledge wherein we are behind our brothers of the Old World; her conviction of the absurdity of our eternal self-glorification as a country, she recorded on the title-page of her "Letters from Abroad," in a motto which we think she might adopt in her opinions of other things with equal truth: "Well, John, I think we must acknowledge that God Almighty had a hand in making other countries besides our own."

It is impossible to read any of the writings of Miss Sedgwick without being impressed with the idea that she wrote not for applause, nor for self gratification, but with a more generous aim, and with a higher ambition. We know of no American author who has done so much to eradicate false notions of domestic education, or of social economy, who has made so many homes happy, and infused such sterling principles with such gentle tones into the popular philosophy. Would that there were more gentle spirits to rise and follow in her steps — to imbrue their own minds first with a love of the truth, the broad, sound, fundamental truth which underlies human prosperity in its widest scope, and then devote themselves to its propagation, with the seriousness and humility of Miss Sedgwick! If they should not all produce works which for their literary merit, but more for their sanctifying influence, future ages will not let die, the thought of the poor whom they have visited and comforted, of the sad homes they have cheered, of the schools they have fostered, and the ignorant they have lured to a love of knowledge, will, as we are sure it does, to gladden the serene maturity of Miss Sedgwick's life, breathe into their reflections,—

"the consciousness of living in
The grateful memory of the good!"

Of Hawthorne we feel at liberty to speak more freely. The example which he himself has set us, in his introduction to "The Scarlet Letter," is of itself sufficient to remove all scruples that we might otherwise have.

On the northern shore of the Stockbridge Bowl, in a spot of unrivalled loveliness, stands a small, uninviting red house with green window-blinds, and with one single pine tree before it. You might pass it at almost any time of the day, and you would think it vacant; the doors would all be shut, the blinds all closed, and that single pine tree would look as sullen as if it were conscious of its loneliness. There would be no path to the gate, and no knocker on the door, and you would immediately conclude that the red house of the two gables was shut against the resort of men, — and you would not be far from right, for there lives Nathaniel Hawthorne.

If, however, on a closer inspection you observed a wreath of smoke curling up from the chimney of the house of the two gables, and had curiosity enough to saunter about the precincts, in hopes of seeing signs of life, until about four o'clock, you would finally hear the door creak, and there would stand before you a middling-sized, thick-set man, with a large, vigorous face, and lying under a profusion of coarse, black hair, a head of massive development. There would be no particular feature in his countenance of especial beauty, except it were his dark and intelligent eye, arched by a very black eye-brow, — yet you would gather from the *tout ensemble* of the expression that it betokened an intensely-working and thorough-going intellect. Were it not that the countenance is relieved and heightened by the vigor and intensity of mental activity, that beams through it, you would think there was something in it very heavy and sombre. If you ever had any hint that there was a vein of rancor and acrimony in his character, you would see no indications of it in his face, unless you fell to imagining what expression that black eye would take, and that heavy eyebrow, and that firmly drawn mouth, when he was belaboring the Custom House officials, or spurring his bitterness against some hypocrite, — who was of course a Calvinist and a Puritan. But while you were making these observations, your hero would raise his eyes from the ground long enough to give you one of those modest but expressive glances which mark the man of seclusion and reflection, and then with a kind of swinging gait which would assure you that he was not used to bustle among the crowds of business or fashion, would wend his way up to the village Post Office.

Mr. Hawthorne, even for a man of letters, leads a remarkably secluded life. He has a few literary friends with whom he cherishes an intimacy congenial to a mind of such cultivation and sensibility, and a friendship which does honor to his heart, but he shows no disposition to mingle largely in society. This aversion to social intercourse has been remarkable in him during his literary career, and even far back into his youth, if we may credit the accounts of his acquaintances. Not only in his private life, but all through his writings, there seems to breathe an unsympathising, morbid spirit, — a spirit that seems to take a satisfaction in keeping itself aloof from those who are guilty of the foibles which it takes a still greater satisfaction in contemplating. This spirit he could never have inherited from his ancestors, else those progenitors of his, who for so many generations "followed the sea," were a strange set of tars! Perhaps all his better sympathies were chilled in those speculations with his dreamy brethren of the Brook Farm Community; perhaps he and Emerson, enraptured with the mystic perfection of their own fantasies, abjured all communion with this our gross humanity; he certainly could not have had his feelings frozen into hate by contact with the genial and sympathizing intellect of Ellery Channing, or at the warm hearth-stone of Longfellow.

Yet, after all, we should be strangely insensate and

ungrateful, if we were disposed to grumble at what may be, in the case of Mr. Hawthorne, but the concomitant of seclusion and literary devotion, or what at the worst is so admirably wrought into piquancy in his writings. The world, and we with them, would be sorry were it far otherwise, and we are perfectly indifferent as to which of the two gables of his red house he shuts himself in, if he will but open the door occasionally, and send forth such volumes as he has of late been giving to the public. But we are not so selfish that we cannot see, or that we would not like to tell Mr. Hawthorne, that our gain is his loss, in one respect at least. We would tell him that the church upon our hill — the church, too, whose walls echoed the almost dying tones of his beloved Channing, in his last public address — is not the sanctuary of asceticism of any kind, and the eloquent sincerity of a believing Calvinist has attractions even for those who have no sympathy with his piety; but the shadow of the occupant of the house of the two gables seldom, if ever, darkens a church door. Doubtless the remains of the Puritan sermons which moaned through the shattered timbers, and pealed through the tree tops of the old manse at Concord, sufficed Mr. Hawthorne for the remainder of his life, or else disgusted him with the idea of anything which by any possibility could savor of Puritan homiletics.

Mr. Hawthorne was born and spent the early part of his life in Salem, that old Puritan city, where the witches were persecuted with such relentless fury; — a city which still, in spite of the cheerfulness of its modern improvements, cannot be dissociated from that gloom which invested it of old, as if the "Gallows Hill," which overlooks it, would never withdraw its shadow. Here, doubtless, he imbibed that fierce hatred for many traits of the Puritan character, which pervade and almost embitter his writings. There is always looming up in the background of his picture — ill protected by the thin tissue of the tale, or rather thrown into bolder relief by its reflected light — some gaunt old snuffler, bigoted in his zeal, hypocritical in his professions, who, notwithstanding that he is at heart the very chief of sinners and almost a rival for the chief of demons, lays all the claims to sanctity to be found in the lankest possible hair, the most fervid quotation of Scripture language, in a voice not wanting the due nasal intonations, — in every respect the devoutest of men, save in his heart, where rankle the worst propensities and the most damnable passions. With a sort of bitter pleasure, and regardless of the rules of warfare, Mr. Hawthorne first stealthily strips him of his coat of mail, and then against his exposed enemy levels a storm of poisoned shafts, barbed with all the skill that a refined malice can invent, that he may have the fierce satisfaction of glorifying in his fall. We can hardly forgive Mr. Hawthorne this assault on the occasional weaknesses of here and there one of those whom, notwithstanding, a long line of children glory in claiming as their ancestry. Bating this one characteristic, which, though it may add to the piquancy of his writings, certainly detracts from their merit. Mr. Hawthorne is one of the purest, most forcible, as well as most graceful, of living English prose writers. His style is splendidly constructed, his language racy and idiomatic, while the magnificent web of his imagery — sometimes reflecting the glance of a metaphor, and sometimes interweaving a long array of analogies into a beautiful allegory, is enchanting beyond description.

Mr. Hawthorne's last published book, "A Wonder Book, for Boys and Girls," contains a number of accurate descriptions of our Lenox scenery. He fitly styles himself "the silent man in the red house." In this book he has worked up six of the classical myths into forms adapted to the capacities and suited to the improvement of the young, — and we think with remarkable success. That he who has furnished strong and muscular food for staid men, can thus cater to the milk loving palates of children, is no meagre evidence of a versatile mind.

"The Scarlet Letter," and the "House of the Seven Gables," have been received with great favor in England, and their author pronounced one of the master magicians of the age, in his province. And notwithstanding the minor charges which we felt bound in justice to lay at the door of "the silent man in the red house" of the two gables, we would have it understood that we cherish the thought of his abode among us with a complacency commensurate with the splendor of his abilities and his renown.

Although Mrs. Kemble is temporarily absent, we still reckon her among our honored residents. Indeed, even if her return was not anticipated at no very distant period, there are few who would be willing to forget the partiality which a lady of such distinguished reputation and undisputed taste has shown to the scenery and other attractions of Lenox. She is remembered as a marked and generous woman; there is not a peasant in the region — however much he may have been startled at her individualities — who has not some tale to tell of her munificence. It was not to be supposed that many of the graver people would look with much complacency on the *port* and demeanor of so singularly spirited a lady, much less on her man-like propensities to driving, hunting, and fishing, and less than all on her man-like attire, while engaged in them. There are many who did not know her, save as a splendid, imperious, passionate woman; they could not love her who knew not also how ardent and generous a nature was hers. That she had extraordinary genius, an inflexible and irresistible will, and a consummate address, every one, who ever saw her, acknowledged; that she had the tender sympathies of a noble nature, the poor by whose bedsides she watched, and to whom she read the Bible in their sickness, will convince you, with many a tearful tale; but those only who knew her as a friend, can tell the full strength of her claim upon their admiration and their love.

But it were both ungrateful and unjust to close these sketches of those whose presence among us has done honor to our village, without paying a tribute to one who devoted his conspicuous talents, and his long and honored life, to its spiritual upbuilding. It very rarely falls to the lot of any community to be under the guardianship of so large-souled and devoted a man as Dr. SHEPARD. With abilities which gave him a towering eminence among his brethren, united with great physical and personal endowments, his power as an eloquent speaker, no less than a vehement proclaimer of the truth of God, stood confessed in the admiration of two generations of men; while his genial piety and the strong flow of his sympathetic ardor, have gained for him even more, to love him and to venerate his memory, than those who admired the breadth of his intellectual view, and the fervor and power of his eloquence. After having long been regarded as a venerable "Father in God," he closed his career of more than half a century of pastoral labor in Lenox, in January, 1846.

"None name him but to praise."

CHAPTER XII.

LAKE ONOTA — AND ITS WHITE DEER.

I SAID, the other day, that Pontoosuc was not quite my favorite, among our mountain lakes. Onota is. This beautiful sheet of water lies in an elevated valley, some two miles west of our Old Elm, whence our matter-of-fact people almost universally call it the "West Pond." You reach it by a few steps from the high road, upon the north or south, but it is almost eremetically concealed from the passenger upon it. If one is a good walker, the better approach is across the fields, between the two. From almost any part of the main street of our village, you can see upon an eminence in the west two twin elms, forming a perfect gothic arch, — "St. Mary's Arch" they call it. Keeping your eye upon this pretty landmark, follow such footpath as you can find; and when you reach it, a few steps farther will bring you to the green and mossy woods upon the eastern borders of Onota.

Of all our lovely groves, none are more perfect than this. Few have so hermit-like a solitude; yet none are so far removed from a desolate loneliness. These shades are sometimes very solemn, but never gloomy; one cannot feel very sad in them, but with a merry company might be very gay.

9*

Around these shores were some of the earliest settlements; and before the intrusion of the white man, they were the favorite haunt of the Indian. A gentleman tells me that in digging into a bed of peat and marl, upon his farm on the west of the lake, he has found, at great depth, stakes pointed artificially, — evidently the remains of wigwams built ages ago, when, perhaps, the marl bed was a lakelet as crystal clear as Onota. Remains of the rude arts of the later Indians used to be found in the neighboring fields; but now they are rarely, if ever, turned up by the plough.

Wandering through the grove we come to the northern extremity of the lake, whence the view to the south is very wild and imposing; I believe it is the fashion for artists and connoisseurs to consider this the best point of view to be had of the lake, — indeed as the best of its kind any where to be found. The peculiar formation of the lake is certainly here displayed to the best advantage, and is very curious. At about one quarter of its length from its northern end, it is divided by a narrow isthmus; the northern portion of the lake being the work of those skillful engineers, the beavers, — who formed it by building a dam across a small stream which still runs through it, overflowing their embankment in sufficient quantities to turn a mill wheel at some distance below. The main or southern lake is fed by springs.

The fringed gentian, the cardinal and other gorgeous wild flowers, grow in profusion at the north of the lake. The more pleasant resort, however, is upon the south, — where, of a dreamy Summer afternoon one can recline in luxurious reveries, as he watches the image of the mountains, sharply reflected in the clear waters; sometimes in the green leafiness of June, sometimes in the melancholy gorgeousness of Autumn, or, better still, when the haze of the Indian Summer invests them with hues of pearly delicacy and richness.

Perhaps, while you look, a broad winged eagle will appear above you, soaring and sweeping in the silent sky till it vanishes into the heavens; or a blue king-fisher will perch awhile upon yonder blasted bough, and then suddenly darting into the water bear away its writhing prey to its hidden haunt. Other gentler birds will sit a-tilt on the lithe green branches — and, if it be in early Summer, serenade your slumberous ear.

Near by, the cattle will stand in groups on a pleasant point of land which runs out into the lake, and which they seem to love better than other spots. It was this point which the Indians called Onota, whence the earlier settlers extended the name to the whole lake. There are a couple of legends about this Onota, perhaps worth the telling. The first is well authenticated, and the other not improbable, as legends go.

The Legend of the White Deer.

There is hardly a country where a deer ever trod in which there does not linger some legend of one or more of these graceful animals, either wholly or in part of a supernatural whiteness. It is a fancy which seems to spring spontaneously in the rich soil of a woodman's imagination. The "White Doe of Rylston," and Bryant's "White-footed Deer," will occur to every one, as instances of the use to which these traditions have been put in poetry. Traditions with very similar incidents and catastrophies are said to exist in almost every tribe of North American Indians, and among others, those of the Housatonic valley.

A gentleman tells me that in the "old witch times," there were no firmer believers in supernaturalisms than the people who lived about Onota; one of whom was his own grandfather. This worthy old gentleman — dead long since, but then a middle-aged man — coming in from an unsuccessful hunt, saw a white deer stooping down to drink, at Point Onota. Instantly his rifle was at his shoulder, but, before he could pull the trigger, his dog howled and the startled deer disappeared.

The marvellous story of the White Deer immediately occurred to him, and it entered into his head that his dog was bewitched, or rather that an old hag who lived in the neighboring woods had assumed the shape of the dog — which, among other devilish freaks, she had the dangerous reputation of being able to do. With never a doubt, therefore, that he was all the while belaboring the old witch, our disappointed hunter belabored his poor beast until the woods howled again. This done, he posted away to the cabin of the old crone and demanded that she should show him her back, on which he did not doubt he should find the marks of the blows he had inflicted upon his miserable hound. Of course the old lady was in a tempest of wrath when she learned the errand of her visitor; and it is believed my friend's grandfather made a retreat more discreet than valiant, under a shower of blows from that notorious article of household furniture which was supposed to serve its mistress the double purpose of a broom by day and an aerial steed by night, and which now answered another very excellent turn.

Another gentleman, to whom I mentioned this anecdote, tells me an aboriginal legend of this same White Deer.

"Long before the Englishmen set foot in the Housatonic valley," he said, "the Indians used to notice a deer, of complete and spotless white, which came often, in the Summer and Autumn months, to drink at Onota. Against this gentle creature no red man's arrow was ever pointed; for, in their simple faith, they believed that with her light and airy step she brought good fortune to the dwellers in the valley. 'So long,' the prophecy ran, 'So long as the snow white doe comes to drink at Onota, so long famine shall not blight the Indian's harvest, nor pestilence come nigh his lodge, nor foemen lay waste his country.' In the graceful animal the tribe recognized and loved their good genius. He among them who dared to harm her would have met swift punishment as a sacriligious wretch and traitor."

Thus protected by the love of her simple friends, year after year, soon as the white blossoms clothed the cherry, the sacred deer came to drink at her chosen fountain; bringing good omens to all, and especially to the maiden who first espied her glittering brightly among the foliage. Finally she brought with her a fawn, if possible, of more faultless purity and grace than herself; and that year more than the usual plenty and happiness reigned round the lake. Not long after this, the first French and Indian war broke out, and a young French officer — Montalbert by name — was sent to incite the Housatonic Indians to join in the league against the English Colonies.

In his sacred character as an ambassador he was welcomed to their lodges, had a seat at their council fire, and listened eagerly to their wild and marvellous tales. Among others he heard the story of the White Deer; and however incredulous of her sanctity, sufficiently admired the descriptions of her beauty. Among those reckless and ambitious adventurers who set up the standard of France in Canada, it was a passion to carry away some wonderful trophy of the forest domain, to lay at the feet of their sovereign. Even the persons of the savages had thus been presented at the Court of Versailles, and royal favor had not been niggard in rewarding the donors of the more unique and costly trophies of barbaric splendor.

It was for such reasons that an uncontrollable desire to possess the skin of the White Deer took possession of Montalbert. He already enjoyed, in imagination, the reward which could not fail him who brought so rare and beautiful a peltry to the splendid Louis.

Not fully aware of the veneration which the Deer received from the natives, he first offered liberal rewards to the hunter who should bring to him the coveted spoil. For half the proffered price the chiefs would, perhaps, have alienated their fairest hunting-grounds; but the proposition to destroy their sacred Deer was received with utter horror and indignation. It was gently hinted to Montalbert that a repetition of the offer might ensure him the fate he designed for the Deer.

But the Frenchman was not of a nature to be so baffled. He had noticed that one of the native warriors — Wondo, by name — was already debased by the use of the white man's fire-water, of which Montalbert possessed a large supply. Concealing his purposes for a time, the adventurer sought out this Wondo, and shortly contrived to foment the poor fellow's appetite to such a degree that he became the absolute slave of whoever had it in his power to minister to his desires.

When the hunter was thought to be sufficiently besotted, Montalbert ventured to propose to him a plan to secure the skin of the White Deer. Depraved as he had become, Wondo at first recoiled from the thought, but appetite at length prevailed and he yielded to the tempter.

Years of unmolested security had rendered the Deer so confident in the friendship of man that when at last treachery came, she proved an easy victim. Before conscience could awaken in the sacrilegious hunter, the gentle animal was taken and slain, and the illgotten fur was in the possession of the white man.

No sooner had Montalbert secured his prize than, concealing it in his baggage, he set out for Montreal; but the legend hints that he never reached the French border, and the beautiful skin of the Indians' sacred Deer never added to the splendors of French royalty.

Among the natives, the impious slaughter was not suspected until the fire-water of the slayer was expended, and a returning consciousness compelled him to confess his deed of horror, and to meet the speedy vengeance which atoned for it.

Long and earnest were the supplications which the

frightened natives sent up to the Great Spirit, that He would avert from the tribe the punishment due to such a crime; but the prosperity of the tribe never again was what it had been, and its numbers slowly wasted away.

Yet it is said that when they had become very few and feeble, a white deer again came to drink at Onota, and that same year the Missionary, Sergeant, first proclaimed the truths of the christian gospel among these hills, and the red Indian learned to know the white man's God.

There are many hints of dim legends like these about Onota, — both of the early settlers and their predecessors. One, who at this day looks upon its beautiful scenery and breathes its pure air, can well feel why life used to cluster thickly around its shores.

There is one little corner of the lake — an open bay overhung by dark woods and covered with lilies, that reminded me one evening, when white mists were gathering over it, of a little German ballad. Perhaps the connection is of the slightest, but it will warrant me in giving a translation of what, in the original, seemed to me beautiful. The Mummelsee is a small, gloomy lake in the Black Forest, near Bâden-Bâden.

Mummelsee: a ballad from the German.

Tho' Mummel's lake is lone and drear,
  Yet there the lilies bright are blooming,
And, bending low, their kiss they yield,
  The wanton breeze of morn perfuming.
But when the night on earth comes down,
And the white moon puts on her crown,
From the dark wave each flower uprises,
Like youthful maids in festal guises.

The winds that whistle through the grove
  Give fitting music for their dances,
While on the shore each Lily-maid
  Through mazy circles deftly glances.
Their graceful forms, how slight, how frail!
How white their robes, their cheeks how pale!
Till the warm dance at length discloses,
Among the lilies, blended roses!

Now howls the wind, now rolls the storm,
  Through gloomy forests fiercely sweeping;
The moon in clouds has hid her form,
  And murkier shades o'er earth are creeping.
Still, up and down the dance goes round
To the tempest tune, on the rough, wet ground,
While the foam on the lake-wave whiter flashes,
As its crests on the shore it higher dashes.

An arm from out the lake is raised,
  A giant hand and clench'd outthrowing,
A dripping head, with sedges crowned,
  With a white beard long and flowing.
Then a voice is heard, with a thunder tone
That echoes afar through the mountains lone,
"Back, vagrant Lilies, to your native waters,
Back to your homes, unduteous daughters!"

The dance is stilled, the maids grow pale,
  'T is sad to hear their fitful shrieking:
"Our Father calls—Ha! morning air!
  Back, then, our cheerless waters seeking!"—
The silver mists from out the valley rise,
And morning painteth gay the eastern skies;
Again the Lilies to the winds are sighing,
Their pale, meek heads upon the waters lying.

CHAPTER XIII.

VISIT TO A SHAKER MEETING.

THE name, and something of the character, of the "United Society called Shakers," is doubtless familiar to you. Everybody has heard of their saltatory worship — an absurd mockery of cheerful devotion — of their doctrine of universal celibacy, of the perfection of their workmanship, the excellence of their husbandry, and the wonderful neatness and order of all that pertains to them. This, however, by no means comprises a complete, or the most valuable view of their character. Understand them rightly, and I think you will find this secluded body of strange religionists one of the most instructive, as well as extraordinary social phenomena, which the world presents. There is something else to be learned among them than careful husbandry, or thorough workmanship — something more worthy of observation than an ungainly garb, or yet more ungainly dance. It is by such strange distortions of the social system that the moralist learns much of its internal nature, — as the geologist determines the internal structure of the earth from its upturned and distorted strata.

I do not, however, purpose to play the moralist, but to give some account of a visit to the Millennial Church, at New Lebanon, and a brief sketch of their organization and manner of life.

Last Sunday I overtasked the generosity of a friend by accepting a carriage seat to visit the church of this strange sect, or rather this unnatural offshoot of christianity. It was one of those mornings we keep forever among our choice memories. Never was balmier west wind than breathed upon us, over the green hills of Taghconic; never was bluer sky, or fleecier clouds, or more heart warming sunshine than ours. We were not now in pursuit of natural beauty; but, off the Berkshire hills, you may wander over many a league of lovely landscape, and find none so lovely as will greet you at every step upon them. "Here!" "There!" "Yonder!" we were continually exclaiming, as one and another espied some exquisite little vista opening up the valley; some fine old tree standing out in relief from the wood; or some clear brooklet meandering awhile by the road side and then dashing down a rocky bed, to hide itself in the ravine below. Now we watched the shadows of the clouds passing, like dreams, over the breasts of the sleeping hills; and now the shimmering sunlight, as it glinted down through the rich foliage with as mellow, warm-colored light as that which gleams through old cathedral windows.

One of our party — a daughter of the West, whom we will in ink christen "Hesperia"— had always some apt quotation to illustrate every scene, and express every sentiment; another such glowing eloquence of lip and eye as continually rebuked the coldness of admiration which matter-of-fact people would have called excessive, if not insane. It was just such a merry, impressible party as one should desire to meet in pleasant lands.

We soon reached the village of the Hancock Shakers, which they poetically call the "City of Peace." It is conspicuous, with its huge round stone barn, — the best model, it is said, to be found for a building of the kind; it is certainly the noblest looking agricultural structure I ever saw. The meeting-house at this place was closed, and the people were going out to hold a "mountain meeting," — a great festival in Shakerdom, of which I shall have more to say, presently. One of the brethren, however, politely informed us that we should be in ample time for the services at New Lebanon, and at the same time gave a glance, which was anything but Platonic, to the ladies.

With this slight glimpse into the Shaker heart, we drove on, — staying a moment, however, to listen to the sound of monotonous chanting which issued from a house where one of the families (a family, in Shaker parlance, is a collection of from fifty to one hundred persons, living in one house, but in nowise related) was engaged in its morning devotions. It was only a doleful, droning hymn, of which we could distinguish no words, — doubtless very far from melodious in itself, but like other such sounds, not without a certain melancholy sweetness, when heard at a distance, in the stillness of a Summer Sabbath.

Ascending the Taghconics, when we reached the "summit" — as the highest point of each road is here called — the broad valley of the Hudson burst upon us, as if by the withdrawal of a curtain. Before us lay outspread its countless farms, its wooded uplands, and the towering Kaatskills blue in the distance. To some of us the scene was not a new one, nor is it by any means the finest in grandeur or variety which can be had of this splendid valley. We saw neither Palisades nor highland shores; the river itself, with its magnificent border of cities and towns, was hid from view. But I know not when I have been filled with emotions of such sublimity, as when looking down upon that wide, populous harvest-laden slope, white with the corn which was to give strength to nations, now lying there in the Sabbath's rest, while the grey old mountains stood above, clad in priestly robes of mist, as if ready to bestow their patriarchal blessing. It was a scene to which the most prosaic heart might well for once yield.

Slowly descending the western slope of the Taghconics, we soon reached the Shaker village of New Lebanon — the capital of the Shaker world — the rural vatican which claims a more despotic sway over the minds of men than ever Roman Pontiff assumed.

We found the broad, level street, between the rambling buildings of the village, completely blocked up with vehicles of all sorts, from Pittsfield and Lebanon Springs. Stage coaches, hacks, barouches, buggies, — every variety of carriage had brought its quota and variety of visitors. Portly citizens in the glossiest of broadcloths and most rubicund of faces, with massive watch seals and heavy, gold-headed canes; hirsute exquisites, redolent of Broadway and *eau de vie;* ladies, radiant in smiles and diamonds; men, eminent in politics, science, and literature; belles, blues, and heiresses; in short, they were a fashionable mob, in most of the paraphernalia of their order. And a queer contrast they made to the place where they were collected; where all ornament was eschewed as the deadliest of sins, and beauty as the veriest of vanities — to be held in corresponding contempt, and studiously concealed under close fitting caps and hideous dresses.

The church is a plain, angular edifice, without tower or spire, some eighty feet long by sixty broad, with its broadside to the street. It is a substantial clapboarded building, painted of a yellowish color, and with a rounded roof covered with tin, which glitters very brilliantly in the sunlight. With its green doors, and its grassy, enclosed court-yard, there is a simple, cheerful aspect about it, which, considering its locality and its builders, has a suspicious likeness to the beautiful.

At either extremity of the front is a green door, labelled, the one "MALES," the other "FEMALES,"— a laconic admonition to visitors, that being at Rome they are expected to do as the Romans do. Accordingly, parting from our lady friends, we entered the portal appropriated to the grosser part of humanity.

The church within is as simple as its exterior promises. A pleasant, airy, unpretending hall occupies the whole of the lower story. Bright green Venetian blinds shade the windows, and about one fourth of the floor is fitted up with comfortable raised seats, for the accommodation of spectators. The remainder is a clear, polished surface, reminding one of the travellers' stories of Dutch housewifery — which is always, indeed, more than rivalled by that of the Shakers. Here are ranged some plain deal benches, without backs. A huge sounding-board overhangs the whole, in order that nothing may be lost of the precious tones emitted beneath it, — precious indeed, for there Heaven vouchsafes to hold direct intercourse with its chosen people.

Several apertures in the upper part of the walls we at first took to be part of an apparatus for ventilation, but they proved to be ear holes for the eavesdropping of the "Lead,"— that is, two male and two female elders, who dwell in inviolable seclusion in the second story of the sacred edifice. These august despots are much addicted to this species of the kingcraft of the First James, — but fortunately the people, in this case, have the advantage of knowing that they are watched.

A door in each end of the hall completed the arrangements, and was attended by a queer looking janitor — a compound of Shaker saint and Yankee sexton. The seats for spectators were nearly filled when we entered, but the rest of the hall was unoccupied, and there was no Shaker to be seen, except the odd looking janitor.

Presently a Shaker in full uniform appeared, and looked around the room with the air of a reconnoitering officer, or more, perhaps, as you may have seen a stage manager or scene shifter, just before the rising of the curtain in a theatre. When this forerunner retired I judged something was about to happen, and, having no seat to lose, went to the door to learn what it might be.

I was not disappointed. The whole Shaker people were moving towards the church in procession, and the effect was very fine, — particularly of the women, who, dressed in spotless white, and moving with a noiseless tread along the quiet valley, reminded me of a procession of white nuns. Indeed, so strongly did the fancy possess me that I caught myself listening for some old melodious chant to break upon the stillness of the air. The company of drab colored men was much less picturesque, but came in well enough to fill up the unique scene, as did also the varnished carriages of the visitors, with their horses listlessly enjoying the morning rest, and the coachman lazily dosing upon his seat;—a more comfortable personage does not exist than your true coachman waiting for his passengers; few have learned so well the poet's lesson, "to labor and to wait." But the procession advanced, and I did not remain to have the romance of my first impressions destroyed, but returned to the hall before they came near.

It was not long before the procession followed, and, after some slight preliminary formula, seated themselves on the deal benches — the males upon the east, the females upon the west, facing each other. It is hard to describe, but easy to catalogue their costume. That of the males consisted of loose trousers, a long, straight vest, and a long, straight, shad-bodied coat, all of drab, and in the fashion of the times of the Revolution. The costume of Houton's statue of Washington, at Richmond, Va., is not very different from that of a Shaker in full dress.

The dress of the women was a long-waisted, narrow-skirted gown, innocent of the abomination of bustle; high-heeled shoes, muslin neckerchief, and close fitting muslin caps, in all cases completely concealing the hair; every part of the women's dress being in most cases of the purest white. Upon the left arm, which is bent at right angles across the breast, the women also carried conspicuously a white handkerchief.

All this is minutely prescribed by the holy laws

given by God at New Lebanon, in the year 1840,—of which "holy laws" I shall have more to say, presently. So much of the Shaker costume, but you can have little idea from it of the odd look of the performers, in the burlesque which was about to commence.

Preliminary to the strictly religious exercises, a slab sided, hypocritical-looking individual came forward to enlarge upon the beauty of decorum; and, after complimenting the "world's people" on their good conduct in times past, to request a continuance of it. Truth to say, not only during the grimly ludicrous dances, but throughout a sermon which was far better fitted to provoke disgust and indignation, than any lighter feeling, the spectators maintained a wonderfully correct deportment.

When this worthy had concluded his speech, a female specimen of elongated acidity went up to certain ladies who had introduced the world's custom of carrying babies into public assemblies, and removed without the sacred walls those delicate proofs of a departure from the cardinal point of Shaker morality. Oh, vinegar faced sister, how often in church and concert-room have we longed for a preventive police force like thine!

Quiet and propriety having thus been provided for, the Shakers prepared to violate both, in the legitimate way. The whole assembly rose and sang a hymn, accompanying the music by a singular motion of feet and hands, which gave the performers a marked likeness to a band of kangaroos. I could catch only two words of what appeared to be the burthen of the song, —"lovely virgins," being ejaculated violently at every turn of the stanza. What with the song and the singers, the eleven thousand virgins of Cologne came forcibly to mind. "Lovely" indeed!

After the hymn, followed a nasal, droning prayer,—not very unlike that of other uneducated sectarians,—full of absurd, but perhaps unintentional, blasphemy; pharisaic self-righteousness, and a sort of half pitiful, half spiteful concern for the souls of their neighbors. Then came more singing in the unknown tongue—an unintelligible gibberish—accompanied by spasmodic dances, promenades, and evolutions, very similar to those with which a country militia company astonishes the village boys. I must confess, however, that the performers here evinced a superior state of discipline, and very excellent drilling.

Often a spirit of enthusiasm is wrought up by these performances, which surpasses all bounds. The actors whirl round with inconceivable rapidity, shout, leap, and finally fall in ecstatic trances; but on this occasion something checked the usual fervor.

The assembly at length resumed their seats, and the same sanctimonious individual who first addressed the meeting, again came forward, and turning his back full upon the saints, began a sermon directed exclusively at the world's people,—or the "children of corruption," as the elect charitably style us.

It is hard to imagine what could have been the object of the preacher, in directing the mass of crudities which he did, at such an audience as that before him. One can hardly conceive the degree of vanity which could lead him to expect to pervert any one of them to the galvanic religion of the saints who sat behind him, twirling their thumbs in complaisant stolidity. On the other hand, the Shaker priesthood are far too shrewd to display wantonly the brazen impudence of this bold defender of their faith. I am inclined to think that although nominally addressing the world's people, our preacher was all the while "whipping the Devil round the stump," and really was working upon his brethren. Perhaps all the while he fancied he heard them saying, "Yea, verily, how our belovéd prophet is confounding these men of vain larning."

And confound them he certainly did, for never was heard a more odious compound of blasphemous assumption, ignorance, and ludicrous sophistry. He began by claiming that the corruptions of the Middle Ages had so far destroyed the authenticity of the Holy Scriptures as to render a new revelation necessary; and such a revelation he claimed that the Millennial Church possessed. He denounced, unmercifully, the errors of the Church of Rome, and proclaimed the Protestant churches children of that scarlet woman, and grandchildren of the arch-fiend himself.

Having thus fairly demolished the religious institutions of the world, he attacked the social, beginning at the holy estate of matrimony, — by way, I presume, of laying the axe at the root of the tree. You cannot imagine the filth which he heaped upon those who live in wedlock. McDowell never described the interior life of the lowest brothel in colors so revolting as those in which this cold-blooded hypocrite painted the holy shrines of christian homes. I do not know but the outward life of this man may be pure, but sure I am that the heart which engenders such things must be full of seething corruption.

There would have been something infinitely amusing in the whimsical deductions by which our theologian maintained his opinions, had they not been so hideously profane. Such wresting the Scriptures by main force, I never before met, in all my experience of theological controversy. For instance, the words of our Saviour, commencing, "I came not to bring peace but a sword," were coolly interpreted into a command that men should sever all the ties of parental, filial, social affection, blot out the sweet influences of family life, and become like the spiritless beings in whom subjection to men of the speaker's kidney had destroyed all of soul that is destructible. In the relations of parent and child, of brother and sister, husband and wife, there are commonly thought to be obligations of some sanctity; but a stroke of Shaker logic annihilated them in a breath: "A man is a man," argued our preacher, "before he is a father, and therefore he may and should eradicate from his heart all affection for his own child, in preference to that of another; a man is a man before he is a husband, and though he may love the woman"— in a Shakerly way, of course — "he must hate the wife." I do not recollect how the case of a child was disposed of, for certainly he is a child before he is a man; but the preacher went on through the whole of the family relations.

The burthen of the whole affair was the praise of celibacy and the abuse of wedlock, — which was treated in a way sufficiently scandalous, not to say indecent. Our philosopher did not, however, wish the human race to become extinct, but he thought it might be propagated in a more decorous and less objectionable mode — which, however, he did not condescend to point out, although we were curious to know. The sort of monster a Shaker "Frankenstein" would create, would be worth one's while to see.

Fatigued with this trash, I diverted myself by studying the faces of the Laity, and the lesson was more easily understood than the sermon. The men did not lack a certain air of vulgar intelligence. There was perhaps as healthful a hue in their cheeks as you will ordinarily see in a country congregation; but the stolid sanctimony of the mass was very repulsive, and the lonely and desolate air of the old men was painful to see. I could not but contrast these last with the venerable fathers of the hamlet whom I used to look upon with so much reverence, in the village church of L., as they sat in their own pews, surrounded by children and grandchildren, or, in the crowded porch, returned the kindly and familiar greetings of their pastor. To those, who have considered well the mellowing influences of whatever reminds us of the vicissitudes of life, it will not appear an indifferent matter that Shaker discipline destroys those distinctions in dress, which mark the mourner and the bride, the young man and the grey-haired sire, — even the matron and the child.

A sad sight was that, of the young girls cut off from all that sheds a charm and halo upon their years of maidenhood. It is some relief, however, to think that many of them will, in good time, recognize the teachings of Mother Nature to be far better than those of Mother Ann, and, exchanging the Shaker garb for a bridal dress, flit away to the Springs — Lebanon Springs, our Gretna Green. Still the sight is sad, for very few of the sisters, in their hideous apparel, show sufficient attractions to warrant a man in making his way to them through the impediments which are here sure to beset the path of true love. Nevertheless, I earnestly recommend any young gentleman romantically inclined, to make the attempt, and so rescue at least one enchanted damsel from the den of these celibate dragons. Be sure there is beauty there, if you can but discern it. But, seriously, the sallow cheeks and the lacklustre eyes bear sad record of the violation of Nature's laws. From seat to seat the eye wanders almost in vain, in its search for a cheek of rose or a sparkling eye; with few exceptions, all is listless, forlorn inanition.

The contrast in physical appearance, between the males and females, is very remarkable, and it is curious that Mrs. Kirkland has noticed one, exactly the reverse, between the priests and nuns of the papal church in Italy. "There is," she says, "a painful difference between the aspects of the priests and that of the nuns, in point of cheerfulness. The priests wear a look which cannot be called anything but sad. They have not the appearance of men satisfied with their lot in life, or who have found the best consolation for its ills. The nuns, on the contrary, — so far as our opportunities for observation have extended, — were more cheerful than most women. The blood mantles in their cheeks; their eyes light up easily; they show you their precious things with an evident enthusiasm; and when you ask them if the recluse life is a happy one, they answer with such warmth and earnestness that you cannot doubt their sincerity. Perhaps it may be that women are more easily satisfied with a round of petty duties. Ambition is not the vice of their sex. The care of the poor and suffering, and the education of youth, fill up their lives and leave them no leisure for repining. With the priests, it is easy to conceive matters may be quite different."*

The reason of this difference is not far to seek; Mrs. Kirkland solves her problem in stating it. The Roman priesthood are men of cultivated minds, — many of them with a hearty contempt for their profession, — some of them burning with the purest patriotism; their aspirations are for something entirely other than their daily steps lead to. Longing, almost hopelessly, for their own and Italy's better day, they should be sad.

The nun has no such fruitless aspirations; she believes in the earnestness of her nuptials with the head of the Church. In her seclusion, she knows little of her country's wrongs; she is cut off only nominally rom social connection; only conjugal love is forbidden her; father, mother, sister, brother, are regarded by her with an affection only the more intense, that they are separated from her. She is often more highly accomplished, more perfectly cultivated than her companions whom she left in the world; she is surrounded by the masterpieces of painting and sculpture; she listens to the masterpieces of music; she may read the masterpieces of at least Italian poetry and eloquence.

* "Holidays Abroad," by Mrs. Kirkland; vol. II, p. 6.

Nor is she confined to "a round of petty duties;" "the care of the poor and suffering, and the education of youth" are surely things very far removed from that. But one issue for the tenderness and sympathies of woman's nature is closed for her, and from more than one of woman's woes she is exempt.

Let us look at the reverse contrast. The male Shaker is generally of the most limited information; he has few or no aspirations beyond a comfortable support in life; the place of patriotism, love, ambition, are all supplied by self-righteousness, and in some by an escape from the responsibilities of life. Had he been left to the ordinary course of things, he would have ploughed, and sowed, and reaped; being a Shaker, he does the same thing, only in rather a more farmer-like manner. He would have eaten, drunken, and slept; and being a Shaker, he is more certain of doing the same all his life, in a comfortable, hearty manner. The main difference in so far, arises from the fact that he sleeps alone, — and so falls into old age lonely, forlorn, and childless. In the heyday of his life, in the ordinary pursuits of his class, animated by superstition and a strong *esprit du corps*, he has all to which he is capable of aspiring. Of course this applies only to the mass. There are men among them of shrewd intelligence, and even of polished manners. One can easily imagine motives which might induce such to bury themselves in the shades of Hancock and Lebanon.

The Shaker woman has a more melancholy lot. Love — "the first necessity of woman's nature" — is dwarfed, in her case, to most unnatural ugliness. She must renounce the natural affections; she must love none but her own unlovable associates. "Her brethren, according to the flesh," she must regard as outcast and vile. Her education must be confined to the narrowest possible limits; "the arts, sciences, and letters, as ye call them," are expressly prohibited, by statute. Her music must be the noise I have to-day described; if she reads, it must be only the senseless jargon of Shaker theology. Her occupations must be of the most petty nature; in the pleasure which suits the busy, fretful housewife, in scrubbing and polishing, she may share to her heart's content; she may and must go through the tiresome routine of every-day duties as our country dames use. But when all is done, the fruit of her labor goes not to comfort or cheer herself, her home, or her family. Food, clothing, and lodging she undoubtedly has, — good, wholesome, and sufficient, — but it is only, whatever it may be called, as the bond servant of the Lead. With no hope of a to-morrow happier than to-day, the Shaker women toil on, cheerless and forlorn; surely, nothing is less inexplicable than their sallow and inane countenances.

The sudden cessation of the speaker's voice, and the striking up of a quick, lively, camp-meeting tune, broke in upon my reveries, and the dance recommenced. Round and round the soulless, joyless rabble went; more spasmodic — more like a band of galvanized corpses — than before. There was evidently a desperate attempt to work up an excitement; but it was quite as evident that the spirit could, by no coaxing or driving, be persuaded to move. Plainly, there was no hope of whirling-gifts to-day. The presence of the faithless men and women of the world had, perhaps, greater effect upon the nerves and tendons of the dancers than upon the tongue of the orator; and, after a while, they gave over in despair, and took up their line of march for their homes, where, it is to be hoped, a substantial dinner awaited them, for the exercise must have given them a harvester's appetite.

Thus ended a Shaker Meeting.

CHAPTER XIV.

NOTES ON SHAKERDOM.

THINKING you may be interested in learning something more of the strange people of whom I wrote you in my last, I have taken the pains to collect such information with regard to them as I could, from reliable sources. I have especially made use of a little book entitled, "Two Years among the Shakers," which was written by one Mr. Lamson. This gentleman, in search of a better state of society, forsook our deformed social organization for the Community at Hopedale; and, not finding there the Elysium for which he pined, flitted thence to the "City of Peace," in Hancock, Mass. Two years' experience quite convinced him that this was still farther from what he sought; and so, with his wife Mary, who had faithfully followed him in all his wanderings, he returned to the world, — more reconciled, it is to be hoped, to strive after perfection with the generation of which it pleased his Creator to make him a part.

However, aside from his disordered social notions, Mr. Lamson is a diligent and shrewd observer, with an honest desire to see correctly, and report fairly what he saw. In so far as he speaks from observation, he is undoubtedly deserving of credit, and his conclusions are generally plausible.

HISTORY.

The "Millennial Church" was founded in the year 1747, by one James Wardwell and his wife Jane, with a few other persons, mostly of the Quaker order. The tenets which they then held were derived from those preached nearly a century before, by certain enthusiasts among the Huguenots, styled the "French Prophets." Until the year 1758 the Shaker Church was in a very inchoate and precarious state, — being distinguished by few of those doctrines for which it is now peculiar.

In this latter year, however, they were joined by Ann Lee — a coarse and illiterate woman — the daughter of one Manchester blacksmith and the wife of another; from the latter of whom she separated, after having borne him four children, all of whom died in infancy. She is represented to have been very intemperate, and in the constant use of profane and obscene language. Yet, by the masculine energy of her mind, she soon acquired a controlling influence in the infant sect, and induced the aged Wardwells to yield up to her the "Lead."

Assuming now the title of Mother, — which Jane Wardwell had before borne, — she introduced the doctrine of celibacy, and organized the church government, under the style of "The Mother Ann, and the Elders with her." Afterwards, reluctantly, as it is said, at the instigation of the Elders, she proclaimed that the Millennium had commenced, and that Christ had made his second appearance upon earth, in her own person. In the year 1774, Mother Ann, with the wealthiest of her followers, found it expedient to emigrate to America, — and arrived at New York on the 16th of August, in that year. By the advice of some Quakers they proceeded at once up the Hudson, to Niskeyund, now Watervliet, where they have ever since maintained a society. In 1780, an exciting revival of religion called them to New Lebanon, where they gathered their portion of the harvest of souls, and established the society at that place, which is now the most flourishing in the world, and the seat of the Chief Pontificate. In that year 1780, the Shaker leaders were suspected of treason, and thrown into prison at Poughkeepsie, but Gov. Clinton immediately ordered their release. This pseudo persecution, however, helped on their cause,— and Mother Ann and the Elders, travelling wherever inducements were held out, established Societies in Massachusetts, Maine, Pennsylvania, and other states.

In 1784, Mother Ann died, — which, it might have been supposed, would put an end to her divine pretensions. She is, however, still regarded as a second incarnation of the *Word*, and revered by all true Shakers, — as the Son is by Orthodox Christians.

Before departing from the world, she had appointed James Whitaker her successor, or rather her vicar, upon earth; and from that day to this, a succession of similar rulers have administered the government, — "bringing the people into order," and from time to time adding new tenets to their creed, and new commandments to their code, dictated, as they claim, by Divine inspiration.

GOVERNMENT.

The Shaker Government is a theological despotism; holding in abject submission the body, mind, and heart of its subjects, — and regulating every thought, word, and action, from the most awful subjects of meditation down to the cutting of the hair and the posture in bed.

The First Elder at New Lebanon, as successor of Mother Ann, is supreme ruler throughout the world, in all things spiritual and temporal; every command issued by him is regarded as emanating directly from Jehovah, and is obeyed with a corresponding implicitness. All other rulers and governments, throughout the earth, are regarded as rebels against the authority of Heaven. Yet they accept the protection of the law of the land, and often appeal to it in their dealings with the world's people.

The First Elder at New Lebanon appoints a Second Elder, and also a First and Second Eldress, — all of whom he has power to depose at will. These four compose the "Ministry," or "Holy Lead." They appoint a subordinate ministry, similarly organized, in every Society of Shakers in the world; and this subordinate ministry is strictly accountable to the "Lead," at the "Head of Influence," but have unlimited power over the laity of their respective charges. In each Family, again, Family Elders are appointed, with power over the members of the household. A Family you must understand to mean, in Shaker parlance, a collection of as many persons as can comfortably live in a house about the size of some of our large factory boarding-houses, — say fifty or more. Thus three grades of despots are established over the saints, from whom they receive prompt and unquestioning obedience in all matters whatever.

You will naturally ask, in what manner such dominion is maintained. The natural machiavelism of the Lead is remarkable. They have some art by which to govern every mind; or, when that fails, to drive the rebel from their fold. Over the great mass, especially of those brought up among them, ignorance, superstition, and an utter inaptitude for self-reliance, are sufficiently powerful restraints; in other cases, favor, flattery, minor offices, and hope of succession to the Lead, operate. Others, again, are broken down men of the world, weary of unsuccessful effort and only desirous of quiet. Fear of hunger here, and eternal perdition hereafter, with perhaps some spiritual pride, controls the mass. Fear of expulsion to the cold charities and weary efforts of the world, induces at least outward obedience from the few.

The Holy Lead live in sacred privacy, in the second story of the church building. They never associate with the rest of the fraternity, but, although when not engaged in official duties expected to work with their hands, they have separate workshops, — one for the males and one for the female Elders, — where the commonalty are never allowed to enter, except when summoned; and even the inferior Elders may never come, unless upon important business. Into the sacred dwelling houses, not even the subordinate Elders may ever enter.

Although dwelling in the church building, the Lead do not take their meals there, but at the house of the

"Church Family," the upper-tendom of Shaker land. Even here they do not dine with the Family; but a table is laid for them, in a separate room, where they eat in solitary grandeur. When they condescend — as they sometimes do — to dine with other Families, the same magnificent state is maintained. On other occasions the Lead visit the Families, when they retire at once to the Elders' rooms. The Family are then collected in the hall; the Lead come forth, are formally introduced, and address the people in a style of official affection, — perhaps not very different, in substance, from that of more polished Bishops.

THEOLOGY.

The Shaker Theology is altogether a new thing under the sun, and may be new again to-morrow or next week — for one of the Elders assured Mr. Lamson that this doctrine of the Godhead was "a growing thing in the world." The Shaker Deity is neither a Trinity nor a Unity, but a Duality, or better, perhaps, a Quartette, consisting of The Father and Holy Mother Wisdom with their son and daughter, Christ and Mother Ann Lee. These last again are the parents of the new or spiritual creation. In like manner they dualise the principal of evil, and derive from it a world full of evil spirits.

HOLY LAWS AND ORDER BOOK.

Formerly Laws and Creed came orally from the Lead, as occasion demanded, and as in all official acts they are supposed to be inspired, all was regarded as of

Divine Authority. But, a few years ago, something more imposing was deemed desirable, and, at the intercession of Mother Ann Lee, God revealed His Laws at New Lebanon in 1840. They are written in twenty chapters, fourteen of which were read aloud by Elder James Whitaker — spiritually, of course, for Elder James died fifty years ago — to the human instrument who wrote them down. The other six were delivered by the Holy Recording Angel, and recorded in the same way. A supplement called the "Order Book," has since been added; it goes more into detail, but is of equal authority with the Holy Laws. A copy of each, in manuscript, is deposited with the Family Elders, and read aloud to the people on Christmas day, and three times on Mother Ann's birth day. For the rest of the year it is kept under lock and key, in accordance with directions contained in the laws themselves.

The mode in which the Shaker God establishes his laws, is the most unique thing about them, and singularly in contrast with the "Thus saith the Lord" of Holy Writ. The Omniscient, we are told, distrustful of His own work, at the close expressly provides that "So these things shall be, if your Holy Lead approve; if your Holy Lead, in their Holy wisdom with which I have anointed them, give them their union," that is, approval, — in which case "Let them affix thereunto their hands and seals;" which was doubtless done.

The Lead may also, at discretion, set aside any Divine Law, — as is often done with regard to dress, and the use of spirituous liquors; and as Mr. Lamson thinks, occasionally in the matter of sexual intercourse.

EDUCATION.

On the subject of education these laws are curiously precise. Something like schools the statutes of Massachusetts insist there must be, even in Shakerdom; and by the Shaker laws it is provided that in them may be taught Reading, Writing, a *little* Arithmetic, a little Geography, and a little Grammar. Chemistry, Philosophy, and the whole tribe of onomies and ologies are sweepingly forbidden, together with the Fine Arts. As some doubts might arise in the minds of a scrupulous teacher, as to how much a "little" of the prescribed studies might be, it is further explained that "it is better to know too little than too much," — in fact, I suspect that the less the better, for the purposes of the Lead. The favored few, who are destined to rule and prophecy, do doubtless, however, go much further. I have some reason to know that Philemon Stuart, the Chief Prophet at New Lebanon, is a reader of the works of Andrew Jackson Davis, and the series of works published by Fowler & Wells, in New York.

GIFTS AND REVELATIONS.

A gift, in the Millennial language, is something, anything which the favored individual receives from some one of the Godhead, some distinguished saint, or, perhaps, one of the prophets. Many great personages in history have, since death, been spiritually baptised into the church, and are counted high saints in the Shaker calendar. Among others, are Napoleon, Tamerlane, Generals Jackson and Harrison, Pockahuntus, and King Philip of the Wampanoags. Generals Washington and

Lafayette are especial favorites, and are often seen by the gifted ones, mounted on white chargers, and keeping guard over the Mount Sinaï in Hancock.

A "gift" may be either moral, as more faith, hope, love, and the like; or it may be the spiritual receiving of some natural object, as clothing, fruit, wine, — in which case the recipient goes through in pantomime the same motions as if he actually received the thing spiritually discerned; instances will be given in the account of a mountain meeting. Sometimes the gift is a revelation in prose or verse, in which case the seer sings or recites it; but it is for the Lead to say whether it is from above or below — true or false. Care is also taken to provide in the holy laws that no times or season shall be set for the fulfillment of any prophecy.

I must give you some specimens of these Shaker gifts in verse. Here is one from "Job of old," to whom it seems the waters of the river of life have not proved quite a Helicon. Few will think them equal to some remarks of his recorded in the Old Testament.

"You 've much to suffer, much to bear,
In body here I know,
But if you 're faithful you shall share
My blessing as you go.
Be wise, my child, in all your way,—
Be careful what you speak,—
Be on your guard, both night and day,
And labor to be meek."

Another, in the unknown tongue:

"O que won wister wa,
We quon questa ka,
Quo con vister we,
Wo zon zane ke,

Que wain wisna quo,
Se nain quisna woo,
We sain win no haw,
Ka ween na na Wah."

Another, half and half:

"Te he, te how, te hoot te te hoot,
Me be mother's pretty papoose,
Me ting, me dance te I diddle um,
Because me here te whities come."

And so on, by the dozen pages.

All are supposed to be sung through the instrument or medium, by the spirit of some departed saint.

From the region in which they originated, and from great similarity in their character, I have no doubt the "spiritual rappings" now in vogue had their root in Shakerism. The Millennial Church have always claimed to hold communion with the unseen world.

MOUNTAIN MEETINGS.

About the year 1841, a special revelation was received, through the "instrument" at Lebanon, commanding all the societies of "our Zion upon earth" to select a spot upon some mountain or hill near their respective villages, for a Most Holy Place of Worship. Accordingly, the brethren at Hancock, following the guidance of an angel, and armed with pickaxes, spades, and like instruments, marched, one day, up the hill which is now called Mount Sinaï, and came to a halt upon the place which the angel designated. Here they at once fell to work, and, having cleared about a third of an acre of stones, trees, and rubbish, graded it in that perfect manner characteristic of all Shaker work.

This plat was afterwards surrounded with a plain, white strip fence, and a lower fence erected around a small space in the centre, in the form of a flattened hexagon. This latter is called the fountain, and is fabled to be filled with spiritual water, for the cleansing of the nations. Within it is a marble slab, some four feet high, with an inscription stating that it was placed there by command of the Lord Jesus Christ, — and much more.

This stone, and the wild processions up the mountain, have given rise to the popular story, that the Shakers one night hunted the Arch Fiend up the mountain, and there having slain and buried him, danced around his grave in triumph. It is not unlikely that in some of their Walpurgis revels they may have performed some such heroic feat — for nothing is foreign to, nor incredible of, Shaker superstition; but if so, it was only a single performance, and not the staple of the mountain meetings; nor has it any connection at all with the marble slab.

I gave you in my last, some account of a common Sunday meeting; these, however, are tame affairs when compared with the riotous spiritual feasts on the mountain tops. These are the great festivals of the sect; old men and children, young men and maidens, are alike elated with the idea of going on to the hill top. All Shakerdom is agog; the strong and healthy walk; the sick and feeble brave the dangers of a venturesome ride up the steep ascent.

Before starting, each person receives a spiritual dress of the most fanciful splendor. A tunic of scarlet, gorgeous with gold buttons, lace, and bullion, together with a full dress of a corresponding magnificence, adorns each individual of the procession. All this, it must be understood, is entirely spiritual, and visible only to gifted eyes. It is, however, donned with none the less seriousness; article by article it is taken from a visionary chest by an Elder, and gravely received by the wearer, — while, to prevent awkward adjustments, two little angels stand near, by way of *valets de chambre*, or lady's maids.

Thus splendidly arrayed, the procession moves up the hill until it reaches the "Walnut Grove." Here they spend some thirty minutes in preparatory exercises, and then move on again, until they reach the holy ground, when each makes seven low obeisances and enters upon it.

These meetings are designed to be peculiarly free, lively, and impressive; here the spirit of the Millennial Church displays itself without reserve, and a special outpouring of the spiritual gifts is always expected. There is preaching, praying, singing, prophecying, dancing, whirling, twisting, and all manner of contortions. The chief attractions, however, are the "gifts,"— of which I shall give you a couple of specimens. Perhaps a sister is "under operations," and exclaims, "Oh! Mother Ann is here, and sends her love to the brothers and sisters."

"What is it like?" asks an Elder.

"Oh! like little bright, shining balls," answers the inspired sister; and forthwith she commences tossing the little airy nothings among the crowd, who all strive to catch them, with the most ludicrous earnestness. Then, perhaps, a brother shouts, "There is sponge and towels in the fountain, for the people to bathe;" and all go through a pantomimic bathing, — much in the style and with all the unction of Charlotte Cushman, in the hand washing scene in "Macbeth."

At noonday a great feast is held. The anointed seers go forth to shake imaginary trees, whence they gather invisible oranges, grapes, figs, and all manner of delicious fruit, — to do which on the Berkshire hills, in a backward Spring, one would say requires a pretty vigorous fancy. The anointed pick up the fruit in baskets, and placing them, with mutual aid, on their shoulders, stagger under the load to the invisible tables, where it is arrayed with other delicate viands prepared in the same way. Around the table are now placed real deal seats, — the imagination, even after going through all this, not being strong enough to sustain two hundred gross weight of Shaker saint.

All being seated, — except the anointed seers, who wait upon the others, — they eat and are filled with ideal food, they drink and are drunken with idcal wine. By enlarging the number of revellers, the description of the Barmecide feast, in the "Arabian Nights Entertainments," would be perfect for a Shaker feast on the Berkshire hills.

The dinner being over, the revellers are called upon to pay their tithes; that is: the gifted ones, being seated at the imaginary table, the others wait upon them, while the same mummery is gone through as before.

With much more of this sort of thing, the day wears out, and the performers return to the matter-of-fact duties of every day life.

I might give you pages more of peculiarities of this sort, but with this brief abstract of only a few of them, space compels me to close.

I beseech you, my philosophical friend, to consider well the phenomena they present.

CHAPTER XV.

THAT EXCURSION TO GREYLOCK.*

YOU have asked me to describe to you my visit of last Summer to Greylock, and I have promised to comply with your request — but now that I have the paper before me, and attempt to fulfil my promise, I am sensible how inadequate words of mine are to describe what I there saw; and I can more fully than ever before feel the truth of those lines of Wordsworth:

"Ah! that beauty, varying in the light
Of living Nature, cannot be portrayed
By words, nor by the pencil's silent skill,
But is the property of him alone
Who hath beheld it, noted it with care,
And in his heart recorded it with love."

To all those who may read this letter I would say — go to Greylock, see it and commune with it yourselves, for no description can give you an idea of the vast reality. I trust, too, that when you go, it may be in company with friends such as those with whom it was my lot to visit the Mountain, — for kindred mind, taste, and feeling are essential in companions viewing together the beautiful and grand, — such companionship, indeed,

* A friend has kindly favored me with this spirited description of an excursion to the most lofty mountain in Massachusetts.

must at all times add greatly to our enjoyment; but under no circumstances is it so much felt, so much I may say of a necessity, as when our thoughts are exalted by gazing on some great work of Nature. And I know of few things which create a more permanent bond of friendship between persons of kindred mind, than being associated together at such times. But to my promise. Greylock is by far the most interesting of all the mountains in our vicinity. It is the highest, and the most frequented, on account of the surpassingly fine view which its summit affords, overlooking, as it does, some of the most varied and beautiful scenery in the northern States. Nor must it be forgotten, in enumerating the claims of this mountain to distinction, that it serves as a sort of everlasting barometer to the whole surrounding country, affording, at all times, a sure guide as to the prospective state of the weather. Seldom does a pic-nic party set off in this region, without first looking toward old Greylock for encouragement; and if, after they have started, they see the clouds gathering around its summit, they delay not to gather up their baskets, and fly with all speed to a safe retreat from the storm which they know is impending. Thus is old Grandfather Whitehead consulted by all the neighborhood, for information as to sunshine or storm; and one thus learns to feel for him a sort of affection, or rather a neighborly feeling, before visiting him and making his acquaintance on still more intimate terms.

The best point from which to start on the ascent of the mountain, is Williamstown, though many choose North Adams. The reason for preferring the former place, is, that the hotels there are better provided with civil attendants and intelligent guides, than at North Adams. On the occasion of our ascent, most of the party went from North Adams, and found much cause to repent of the choice, — while a few, who differing from the main body, went up from Williamstown, fared much better than we did; and in the foregoing remarks, therefore, I merely give the result of our own experience.

The pathway up the mountain side is rough, but filled with beauty; and some of the openings in the woods almost persuade one that the days of fairy gambols are not yet past, but that in these spots, in these very rings of fresh, green grass — so fresh and green that they seem just to have awakened from their Winter sleep — the elfin revels must still be nightly held. One little wild wood circle I shall never forget, formed by fir trees so densely shaded with thick foliage as to exclude a single peep from the bright face of Sol; while the grass thus growing was of a light, moss color, of that peculiar green seldom to be found, except in small tufts, by a shady brook side. And then the silence and repose of the place had the effect of awing one, as it were, and making one superstitious, in spite of one's self. A shout from our party in advance disturbed our reveries, and no doubt put to flight the elves themselves, who were at that moment coming to occupy their room of state, — for I feel sure that had we remained only a little while longer, we should have seen more than the pen of the author of "Pilgrims of the Rhine" has yet been able to describe, of forest fairy gayety.

We follow the sound of voices from our friends ahead, and on coming up to them are surprised into forgetfulness of the beauty we have regretfully left, for here another scene bursts upon us, as we turn a little aside from the pathway, and, like "Aladdin, or the Wonderful Lamp," we leave one garden of enchantment only to enter another of greater beauty. Oh, this world of ours! how filled it is with objects which elevate and ennoble our thoughts and affections, — if we but seek for them where we ought! Amid God's works how sure are we to feel.

"O God! O good beyond compare!
If these, Thy meaner works, are fair,—
If thus Thy bounties gild the span
Of ruined earth and sinful man,
How glorious must the mansions be
Where Thy redeemed shall dwell with Thee!"

The sun is getting low, and we have still a long steep to climb; so, after we have refreshed ourselves with a drink from a rill of sparkling clear water, we begin our ascent with renewed zest. The beauty about us sufficing us for food, — for, save our sup of Adam's ale we have tasted nothing since an early breakfast, at starting, — totally is the world below us now forgotten. Dinner is supplied by our pass-word, "Excelsior." Some of us linger to gather the wild flowers that are growing plentifully about us, and constantly, by their beauty, beguile us from our path; suddenly we are startled by shouts which echo through the wood like the yells of the red men, and one of our party, with the agility of a well trained sailor (as he was) soon ascends the trunk of a tall tree, and from a seat which appears to us dangerously insecure, echoes shout for shout, till the remaining few of our party, who had come by way of Williamstown, make their appearance; and as they stop to tell us of the good dinner which they partook of at that place, we begin to feel a degree of curiosity to see what the contents of the baskets with which they are well provided are; so, casting our glance forward, we resolve not to turn to the right or left till we gain the mountain top,—nor with this resolution are we long in so doing.

The scene below us is somewhat dimmed by an August evening's haze, which mellows, though it circumscribes, our view, and adds beauty to what was already too beautiful for description. Far off in the distance we see the hills around our own home mountains, as we call them there, but here appearing as gentle undulations, above the otherwise level surface of the ground. Still farther off and still more dimly seen, rises the range of the Kaatskills, with the noble Hudson mirrored at their base. Fill up the picture with a fertile country, dotted with villages and mountain lakes, and beautifully interspersed with woodland, and you have, if your imagination is sufficiently vivid, the scene that lay before us. Silently we gaze and drink in the beauty by which we are surrounded on all sides, till the first impressions of awe and wonderment having in a measure subsided, sly, furtive glances are cast, by the less romantic of our party, towards the baskets which have been companions of our ascent. Soon more active measures are taken, and the claims of hunger now fairly prevailing over us all, we sit down to a supper which the gods and goddesses on Olympus might have envied. Oh, the luxury of a good appetite, and food to satisfy it!

Night is now coming on, and all objects about us begin to have a shadowy, spectral appearance. So a large fire is lighted under a giant stump, and we gather about it, each one indulging, like Ik Marvel, in his own reveries. At length the moon begins to rise, and as her silver sheen appears above the horizon, we grow eloquent, and her potent spell brings out our poetical as well as romantic thoughts. Absent friends are remembered with a sigh, and as we turn to those next us, to share our thoughts, we feel that "mind may act on mind, though bodies be far divided."

The moon, as if conscious how intently we were watching her, rose more majestically than usual, and the light clouds, as they coquetted about her, had more beauty and assumed more variety of shape than we had ever before observed in them. Here we sat till long past midnight, and so intensely were we enjoying the wildness of the scene as to forget that sleep was "Nature's kind restorer." But some of the more prudent of our party urged us to seek rest. Retiring, therefore, to the Tower (a ricketty structure) on the mountain top, we betake ourselves to the so called *rest*, and a more ludicrous scene never presented itself to my mind, than that of our party, now prepared for sleeping during the remainder of the night. Some sitting upright, against the sides of the building; some stretched upon the planks of the floor, which had been raised so as to form a sort of inclined plane; some with their hats drawn over their faces; some more careful to preserve the line of beauty and grace, were drawn up like a cat in a chimney corner, thus exhibiting the effect of the double curve; while a few, too merry for sleep, remained standing, lookers-on in this strangely sorted bed-chamber. A dim light from one candle served to render visible about enough of each figure to distinguish it, and to throw out the evident discomfort of the sleepers, at resting in so rude a place. But how absurd it is, when parties go on such wild excursions as this one was, to expect reserve, or any of the etiquette of refined life.

The morning soon dawned, and, to our great disappointment, the sunrise was obscured by a heavy mist. Yet we were amid the clouds, and had the rain poured down a deluge, it had not damped more than our clothing, — for, with spirits gay as larks, we ascended to the top of the Tower, so as to obtain a better view than we had been able to get, on the preceding evening. But the mist continued to roll along the valley below, and the clouds to envelope us above, for some time; gradually, like a dissolving view, the vapory veil begun to be withdrawn, and the sunshine to illuminate and animate Nature. "Glorious! glorious!" resounded on all sides; and glorious indeed was the scene, as the sun suddenly revealed the world of beauty below us; — dense masses of clouds and vapor, rolling along and assuming in their changes all forms and hues, fantastic as well as grand.

Here we see a cathedral, with the light streaming through its colored windows; there the Colosseum; and again a mass of cloud, so gloriously gilded by the morning rays as to make it too beautiful and grand to be compared to any work of man, or earthly object; and we could have wished to linger there always, watching the Protean changes as they passed before us.

But would our feelings have remained as joyous as they then were? The air seemed truly to have a most exhilarating influence; and could our temperance friends have seen us then, they might almost have been induced to frame a new "Maine Law," placing mountain air on the same footing as intoxicating drinks. Happily, however, we felt no ill effects, as a consequence of this new phase of intemperance, but partook of a hearty breakfast, with an appetite and relish such as only mountain air can give. Our chickens were broiled on red-hot stones, a worthy divine acting as chief cook on the occasion; and the ashes and charmed coals which cling to them, and the primitive fashion in which we were obliged to eat them, only served to make us enjoy the meal with greater zest and mirthfulness.

After breakfast we began our journey homewards, yet, like Lot's wife, casting many a lingering look behind,—and at each step down our steep pathway, losing some of our gay-heartedness; for we felt that we were going back to the world, with its iron rule which cramps and confines our best and purest feelings. But at home again, home comforts about us, and amid the usual routine of life, we remember our journey as a pleasant pause in life, a shrine for memory to return and refresh itself at, when cares and trials make us weary.

Again I would say, go to Greylock. "Commune with your own heart, and be still."

CHAPTER XVI.

ABOUT OUR CATTLE SHOW.

THE Festival of all festivals, the two days for which, in the opinion of our rural population, all other days in the round year were made, are those of the Cattle Show and Fair of the County Agricultural Society. This is the shining goal of the year's race. Dreaming of a silver cup, or at least "honorable mention," at the great anniversary, the farmer tills his soil, tends his flocks and herds, and is careful for many things, in sunshine and storm. For the same momentous occasion the busy fingers of his wife and daughters are plied,—while in the dairy, cleanliest receptacles are filled with balls of golden-hued butter, and cylinders of odorous cheese. In chambers, too, quaintly variegated needle-works bud and blossom, and snowy webs issue from the antique loom.

Nor do the taper fingers of more dainty ladies disdain to contend for the silver spoons; while retired gentlemen of fortune take a notable pride in the display of luscious fruit and mammoth vegetables.

The village beaux prize the day as an occasion for the exhibition of superior gallantry; and the village magnates aspire to the offices in the gift of the Society as no small distinctions in themselves, and possibly—

13*

pardon the suspicion — as stepping-stones to more substantial honors. Few among us but are at least amateurs in agricultural affairs, so that when the great festival of Ceres approaches, our mountain Microcosmos is all agog with excitement.

The country around is in a ferment of preparation. Now is the harvest of the village tailors; now the paraphernalia of the village belles is cunningly renovated; ah! if we could take a sly peep beneath the arcana of the fair artificers' hearts, what murderous designs might be revealed! I think I see them now, amid a wilderness of chintz, and delaine, and calico, and ribbons, — a smile in their eyes and a blush on their cheeks, planting a grace here, revealing a seducing luxury there; sewing a Cupid into every fold, and preparing a snare in every treacherous ribbon. Ah! wicked demoiselles!

Long before the appointed day, partners are secured for the ride to town — not without coquetry, heart burnings, and, it may be, bitter tears in secret places. There is much significance in this excursion to the fair; it is our sweet St. Valentines, when the gay rover takes occasion to signify he shall roam no more. Then, if there chance to be some deserted rival, comes the rush of hot passions, — for, with all the holy calm we prate of, they are as rife in the veriest hamlet on our hills, as in any city of the land. Let him who feels the hot hand of passion on him, thank God if he can fly to crowds and the mad whirl of the city, and so escape the demon — but tremble if he alone must in solitude combat the fiend, with the cold stars above him, from which no angel will descend to his aid, and only the calm lake near, which seems to invite to rest. God forgive him if he seek it there!

Well! what with their mutual delight, and the envy of rivals, the happy couple *are* happy, and you — if you chance to meet them jogging cosily along the road — do not smile too disdainfully, but consider, weddings, and their interminable line of consequents, are likely to be the end of it. Odd! is it not? Out of the rustic amour, at which the high-bred, high bedizened Nothing smiles, come Robert Burns, Oliver Cromwells, Daniel Websters, with all their mighty words and deeds.

But our festival approaches, and the bustle around us is increasing. The weather gets to be a subject of deep interest; almanacs which predict "much — rain — about — this — time," are in ill repute. Weather-wise old ladies, who love to prophecy smooth things, are in high favor; while all vinegar-faced crones are looked upon with a regretful reminiscence of the good old laws against witchcraft.

In the week preceding the Cattle Show of the present year, more eyes were turned heavenward than usual — without, however, any extraordinary amount of piety. There were alarming portents in the skies; an ugly halo encircled the moon; mists hung dubiously about Greylock; fearful things were told by the weather-lochs of the Taghconics; the gathering clouds flaunted angry "mares' tails" far up the western sky; every thing foretold a storm, and the storm did not fail to come.

On the day before the Fair the rain fell in torrents; and the next morning dawned dim, dreary, and drizzling, with an occasional brisk shower, by way of enlivenment. Yet the town was already filling up with visitors. All the preceding day you might have met frequent upon the road little droves of fine oxen, beautiful Juno-eyed cows, and, led by a ring in the nose, bulls of celebrity, with an air of surpassing obstinacy. You might have passed, as well, uncomfortable looking muttons, of enormous fleece, packed in rough, wooden cages; or, you might have stared at some marvellously prolific sow, surrounded by her progeny.

> "Trigenta capitum fœtus enixa jacebat;
> Alba solo recubans, albi circum ubera nati."

All night long such pastoral processions tramped the muddy road, and increased on the dismal morning of the first of October. At an early hour, venerable ancestral vehicles and modernly ingenious contrivances for locomotion, of the oddest possible kinds, began to dump down squads of dripping passengers all about the streets. Hardy belles, with skirts tucked up in liberal folds, exhibiting something more than ancles, strode fearlessly through the mud, while their gallants followed after, with many a rueful glance at their bespattered broadcloth. Those who brought wares betook themselves to the Society's halls, to superintend their arrangement; mere pleasure seekers — miserably mistaken pleasure seekers — went strolling lugubriously about, or congregated dismally in the steamy parlors of the hotels.

But the day was not to be all so gloomy. At noon the clouds rolled darkly away over the Hoosac, and the sun burst gloriously forth upon the drenched earth.

Prettier faces and neater forms began to appear among the crowd, and, now and then, a dashing equipage, warmed out by the sun like a butterfly, rolled along the street. We followed the living current to the centre of attraction, — the show of cattle, — where, stationed around a large field, we found our four-footed friends of the road ruminating as composedly as if in their native pastures. The equanimity with which they received alike the criticisms and encomiums of visitors, was matter for our especial admiration. One would wish to divine, from their quiet and meditative air, what they thought of all the pother about them.

The nice points of the juries of award were about as intelligible to us as the jargon of a Shaker psalm; nevertheless, we ignorantly admired the sturdy forms and brawny necks of the bulls, the distended udders of "the milky mothers of the herd," and were duly astonished at the marvellous obesity of the swine. The lithe limbs and glossy arched neck of a splendid stallion, gave occasion to my companion to indulge in a series of poetic rhapsodies, after the manner of Job, — to which I listened in more humble imitation of the same patient patriarch, although, truth to confess, my own imagination was totally absorbed in the contemplation of certain delicate suckling pigs, that were pictured vividly to my fancy, at the culminating point of their brief existence, with a lemon in each mouth and other appropriate surroundings. It was evidently time to dine.

SECOND DAY.

On the bright and beautiful morning of the second day of the Fair, we again sallied forth, in search of adventures. The streets were densely thronged with all sorts of people, seemingly like ourselves, with no very definite notion of what they were after; —

> "Like a flock of sheep,
> Not knowing and not caring whither
> They come or go — so that they fool together."

My memory is mazed with the recollection of that motley crowd. The representative from Peachem, with gingerbread under one arm and "umberell" under the other, jostled the gloved and caned exquisite from Broadway; and the traveller who could contrast this with the great fairs of Europe was favored with the opinion of the youth whose eyes had hardly peeped over the Berkshire hills. Here and there, men famous, the world over, in politics and literature, went about moralizing, perhaps, — or, more likely, watching that most animated part of the scene,

> "The lassies with sly eyes,
> And the smile settling in their sunflecked cheeks,
> Like noon upon the mellow apricot."

Oh, those sly-eyed lassies! There was one of them, — a most fairy-like creature, with such a delicate and taper waist, with such a foot and ancle, with such an aristocratic face and air, as would have furnished Willis a model for a dozen countesses. I set the owner down in my own mind as the daughter of some village clergyman, or at the very least, of the 'Squire, — and lingered near, hoping some one might pass who could present me; or if that failed, that I might catch some silvery syllables from those lips that curled so like a red rose leaf, — for I confess to having been a little, just a little "struck." But no one seemed to know her, and for a wonder she kept silent.

But at length she spoke. Ye gods! such words! — Turning to a friend, she exclaimed, — shall I repeat it?

"I say, Sall; d'ye 'spose Jim's sold all that cider o' his'n? Goll darn him!"

Do you recollect the scene in "Faust," where the hero was so much disgusted with his fair partner, because —

> "A red mouse, in the middle of her singing,
> Sprang from her mouth."

And how Mephistophiles replied, —

> "That was all right, my friend,
> Be it enough the mouse was not grey;
> Do not disturb your hour of happiness
> With close consideration of such trifles."

My mouse *was* grey, and no trifle at all. Think of it; that odious sentence leaping out of the prettiest little mouth in the world, and suddenly putting an end to a full half hour of wasted affection! I wish I knew the name of my charmer; I am sure it would be a talisman against all such spells in the future.

But to return to our motley crowd, through whom, by dint of determination we pressed our way and took our stand upon an open common, near the Railroad Dépôt. Here booths, stalls, tents, merry-go-rounds, and raree shows had sprung up in the night, like so many mushrooms. Babel and Vanity Fair! Such a discord of tongues and chaos of merchandise one does not often meet. It seemed all the pedlars, from Quoddy head to Byram river, had met in convention. So many shining, twinkling eyes, oily tongues, nasal twangs, "tews," "dews," and "yeous" I did not believe could be concentrated on one little acre of ground. If you think "Sam Slick" a caricature, I beg you will visit this common at our next cattle show. But, on second thoughts, if you are over sensitive about your nerves or your pocket you were better away; for, escaping from a vender of Shakspeare, Milton, and "Venus in Boston," you are beset by a villainous smelling compound, known — on this occasion only — as "oyster stew;" flying thence, as for your life, you fall upon the razor-strop man, and finally, having run the gauntlet of pedlars, showmen, and auctioneers, you take desperate refuge in the jaws of some gigantic show-tent — as we did in one where, a stupendous hand-bill informed us, could be seen all the notabilities of the day.

A "York shilling" procured us the entree and an introduction to a waxen crowd of horrors and heroes, very distinguishable, the one from the other, by the aid of labels.

Coming from the showman's tent with the delightful consciousness of a well-spent shilling, we found the people moving towards the scene of the ploughing match, which was to take place on a field some two miles distant. This is the most exciting part of the festival; the scene has all the interest of the race ground. Upon this arena the strength and training of the best cattle in the county are tested, and the skill and coolness of the flower of our ploughmen are displayed, before dames whose favor is quite as well worth winning as that of any who ever, in chivalric tournament, inspired blood guiltiness. The scene of the contest is very brilliant and imposing, yet this year we did not go to witness it; but while it was passing, preferred to listen to a little story of simple and unhappy love, which happened in connection with one of these ploughing matches, many years ago.

Ralph, the Farmer.

In a sunny nook, among the hills of a neighboring town, lived, many years ago, a young farmer, "the only son of his mother, and she a widow." His patrimony was small, but admirably cultivated. In the whole valley was no better husbandman than he; and you looked in vain for greener fields, tidier barns, and sleeker cattle, than those which called him owner. The little brown cottage under the elms was the envy of all romantic travellers who passed that way.

It was indeed a pretty cottage; any kindly, loving, simple people could have lived there, as did the widow and her son, very happily. Not that Ralph — that was the son — did not think it at times a little lonely; but then it was not with that desolate solitude which now pervades the spot, but with a half pleasant loneliness, sweetly suggestive of future companionship. No bachelor is half so incomplete a being as your farmer; no young man half so matrimonial. Invariably the first thing he does, upon coming into possession of himself, upon his twenty-first birth-day, is to look around—if, indeed, he has not already done so—for some fair hands into which he may at once surrender his new and uneasy freedom. A true farmer makes the best lover in the world, and a still better husband. I mention this for the benefit of any young lady who may, at the present reading, be balancing in her heart a whole souled man against stiff dickeys and patent leather boots.

Ralph was no exception to the general rule, but rather a notable example of it. His great, earnest, warm heart was from childhood continually seeking out something on which to bestow its exuberant love. There was not a human being about but had a corner in his affection; not an animal, a tree, a flower, nor shrub, upon his farm, but his soul twined itself around it. His heart even yearned towards the grey rocks, and he never cut down the bright flowered thistle without a sigh.

No wonder that when Ralph came to the district school he should feel a kindly thrill toward the rosy cheeked little maidens upon the opposite benches. It was characteristic of Ralph, that, whatever was beautiful to the eye, his soul yearned towards it with a devotion that would perceive no inward defect. His old teacher said, years afterwards, that he would sit for hours watching the piles of golden clouds in the west; and that he cared more for the green and golden streaks upon an apple than for its melting flavor. It was an unfortunate omen, that no poisonous flower was shunned by him, if only its hues were fair and silken.

When Ralph finally fixed his heart upon one object,

he was guided by this same fatal love of beauty. It chanced that just across the little valley stood the mansion of the great farmer — the colossal rich man of the neighborhood, who was always addressed as the "'Squire," and, moreover, by service in the councils of the Commonwealth, had obtained a right to the prefix of "Hon." to his name, upon newspapers, letters, pub. docs., and all post-office matter whatever. This gentleman had a daughter — one of those marvels of beauty which now and then electrify a county. The wrinkled gossips, who were fair and young with her — whose bosoms were full and white when they used to thrill with envy, to hear her praises — these gossips, so old and withered now, so young and glowing then, speak, even at this day, of the charms of MARIA with an exaggeration of praise which reminds one of the hyperboles in which the old poets describe their mistresses. The imagination strives, painfully, to lift the curtain of faded years to look upon her loveliness. But the tide of time reveals only, now and then, a fitful gleam; as the water, stilled for a moment, might reveal the placid countenance of the drowned maiden beneath, and then again distort it with its ripples. Yet, even so, we feel something of the beauty which moved our grandsires.

That Ralph should fall madly in love with such a being, was as natural as that his fruit should ripen when the sun shone upon it. Looking upon the matter lightly, there was no prudential reason why he should not. The lady was rich, beautiful, and virtuous. The father, "for all his greatness," was a bluff, hearty, generous old man, with a determined liking for Ralph, which put all opposition from that quarter out of the question. Indeed, as it afterwards turned out, he had set his heart upon having Ralph for a son-in-law. Maria smiled quite as sweetly upon her suitor as even a loving woman should. It would have been strange, had not the tongue of envy whispered that she was doing quite her share of the wooing; indeed, I think I have heard that shrivelled slander hissed by thin and bloodless lips, that, perhaps, had breathed it in their days of cherry ripeness.

The engagement was looked upon as a settled thing, by all the world, — that is, by the half hundred families who formed the hamlet. Worldly prudence and true affection, for once combined, it really seemed as though the course of true love had at last got into a smooth channel.

Doubt all facts which contravene the philosophy of Shakspeare and the ages! You must have known women with a wealth of loving, melting smiles at perfect command, that look so natural and heart-born you would sooner doubt your own senses than their truth; with an eye which holds you in a spell you would rather perish of your faith than break. You must have met such — everybody does — though you could not comprehend them, could not, by any analysis, separate the fair show from the ugly reality. We call such, with as much truth as triteness, "fascinating." Heaven be your help if you ever feel their power upon you! —You were better in the grasp of the wild Devil!

Yet under such fascination was Ralph; such terrible power had Maria, — although she was probably unconscious of it, when she first began to wind her meshes, like the coils of a beautiful serpent, around the heart of our poor Ralph — alas! too happy to be so enfolded. It is not unlikely she deemed she was employing only the innocent arts by which a maiden seeks to obtain a lover, and thought that by and bye she would settle down into a quiet, staid little wife. But flattery had already begun to do its work in her bosom; vanity surely, and not slowly, was becoming the moving spring, the living principle of her existence. In most girls it would have been content to display itself in some knackeries of dress, some prettiness of accomplishment, or at most, in some teasing of their lovers, to show their power over them. But Maria was not an ordinary girl; she had genius — I might better say a demon — in her.

Daily and systematically she displayed her real power over, and her feigned contempt for, her lover, — while she continued to bind him yet closer to her. I do not know that she deliberately determined to continue this course for months, but she found her daily pleasure in it, and had too little virtue ever to bring the day of reform nearer than to-morrow. Ah! if none did evil but those who resolved to lead a life of sin, this would be a pure world of ours. It is the day laborers in Satan's vineyard who do the work.

All the village — except the unsuspecting Ralph and the 'Squire — were familiar with the character of Maria. The village dames, firm friends of Ralph, shook their heads sadly, and prophecied that no good would ever come of such a wooing; the young men murmured indignantly that the frankest and best heart among them was the victim of a selfish coquette; even the minister, who for many years had taken a genial interest in the loves of his parishioners, took Maria seriously to task, for her sinful follies; but in vain.

Matters went on in this way until the Fall, when Maria's brilliant attractions procured her an invitation to pass the Winter in the city, with Mrs. N., a relative, who wished a country beauty, to add piquancy to her *soirées*. The young people parted as lovers part, with some tears, some pretty protestations, and probably a few or more kisses, — such is the custom, I am told.

Months passed away — weary, anxious months for Ralph; for the post brought few letters from Albany, while scandal whispered many unwelcome rumors of Maria's course of life there. Indeed, to let pass other matters, one cannot imagine a society better fitted to foster her darling vice of vanity, than that which thronged the gay saloons of the dashing Mrs. N.; the more so, when we remember that the giddy girl was set up there for the sole purpose of receiving the scentless incense of fashionable homage.

But the Spring came, and with it Maria's return to the country. The lovers — shall I still call them so?— met; met as they had parted, for one had the same ready smile, and the other the same confiding heart.

It was a delicious Summer evening — one of those twilights when the good God pours out his love visibly over the earth, and summons yours to meet it; when you send forth that love, unmindful that it can anywhere meet that which shall turn its sweetness to gall; when, if by chance, you think of sin and hatred and sorrow, it is as of things pertaining to another sphere, with pity for whose inhabitants your heart is yet more softened. It was on such an evening as this, that Ralph spoke of his loves, his hopes, — hardly of his fears; how should he, in such a world of hope?

That was an hour for a true woman's nature to display itself. Had she buried herself in the ashes of coquetry; had she been wandering in a maze of fashionable flirtations; had she wrapt herself in affectations as in a garment,— now was the hour to cast off the delusive shows and appear in native truth.

Ralph, in the deceitful light of that smile and that hour, expected a full outgushing of returned affection. There he was wrong — that he had no right to demand — although, after the parting and meeting kisses, it was, after all, not unnatural that an unsophisticated young man should have been led into error on that point. What he was entitled to, in default of the other, was a plain, kind, unmistakable rejection. He received neither; plainness was neither in Maria's nature nor her purposes. She smiled, more sweetly than ever; looked all a lover could ask, "But really she had not thought of how far this matter should be carried; she had been content with enjoying the passing hour of innocent love" — here she smiled yet more sweetly — "but its present joys had been too seducing to allow a thought for the future;" and much more sentimental falsehood of the same kind.

Both were silent for a few moments, when Maria, as if struck with a new thought, exclaimed: "You know how much my father admires your skill as a farmer — I, too, am not insensible to it; carry off the first prize at the next ploughing match, and I will be yours."

A strange condition this seemed to Ralph, and a poor return for long years of affection, bestowed as unreservedly as his had been; but he was too proud to remonstrate, and, perhaps, too much enamoured to refuse the challenge. But we may ask, was this a maidenly device to cover the surrender of a heart already won? Was it a freak of ill-digested romance, or a plan to minister to a woman's vanity? We may hereafter see.

September came, and with it Mrs. N. came to visit the "Squire," and to attend the "cattle show." At the same time, two or three young men from the city took up their quarters at the hotel of the neighboring town, to the great profit of the livery stable and the bar. Their jaunty vehicles were seen daily at the gate of the old farmer, to his not small annoyance; and the villagers thought the noises they raised, on their late return to town, were not a little disreputable.

At last the day of the contest came. Ralph drove his team confidently upon the field, and looked anxiously around the crowd to catch a glimpse of his mistress. She was not with her father, in the old fashioned family coach; but, after a weary search, his eye found her seated in one of those jaunty vehicles which he so cordially detested, and by the side of one of those dandies whom he detested still more. A pang of jealousy for a moment shot through his heart; — it would have been sharper could he have heard the bitter jest she at that moment bestowed upon her "barn-yard knight." But the signal for the contest was given, and Ralph was at once absorbed in its excitement. I have not space to describe it; enough, that Ralph won, and, receiving his prize, set off at once in search of his mistress — as he, in the honest simplicity of his heart supposed — of his affianced wife.

The end of our little story will not seem improbable, to those who know, as I do, the tender, proud, but sensitive hearts, which beat under the broad breasts of our mountain farmers. With imaginations nurtured among the most romantic scenes of Nature, — often by familiarity with the most touching works of genius, their love often approaches the highest poetic ideal, — almost always transcends the conventional bounds of city "affairs." Such, at least, was that of our friend Ralph, whom we left in eager pursuit of his mistress.

That evening the widow was sitting by the table, upon which the evening meal was placed in readiness; sometimes casting a glance, from the window, down the road, and at intervals bursting into a hymn as cheerful as that of the kettle that sung cheerily over the fire. "It is getting late," she said to herself, "Ralph is late, to-night; he must have stopped at the 'Squire's. Ah, he stops long. Well, well, never mind, it will not be so, by and bye;" and again the good mother smiled cheerfully, — for the widow was much given to a cheerful smile, and a word in her own ear, when alone.

"Hark!" she continued, still to herself, "there's a step upon the stoop, but it cannot be Ralph's." The widow knew the firm, strong, elastic tread of her son, as well as she did his open, manly countenance. No; this could not be his, for it was a halting, aimless gait, dragging itself along, with a clumsy and uncertain purpose. And yet, when the door opened, it was Ralph who entered. Still, it hardly seemed him, — so spiritless, with that wandering, lacklustre eye, that vapid air, those graceless, listless limbs, and not a word for his mother.

"Ralph! Ralph!" she exclaimed, springing towards him, "you are ill! What ails you? What has happened? You have worked too hard in this strife. You have lost the prize?... It was cruel; but no matter, Miss Maria will love you as well without it. Ralph! Ralph! why don't you speak?"

"Miss Maria can't love Ralph," he replied, in a drawling, idiotic tone; "Ralph is only a poor clodhopper."

We leave the distracted mother to be driven slowly to the knowledge that her noble-hearted, high-minded boy had become a brain-sick idiot.

Ralph had, after long search, found Maria at the hotel, where her gay friends were rallying her on her promise to Ralph, — playfully insisting that she was now in honor bound to marry him. Ralph entered the room just in time to hear the reply, in an irritated tone:

"Marry him! — No. Sooner one of the steers he drives, than the awkward clodhopper!"

It was more than enough.

The good old 'Squire insisted on taking Ralph and his mother to his own home, where the latter soon died. It would have been cruel to confine the harmless imbecile within walls, and he was permitted to wander from house to house, among the hills, always meeting a kind welcome at the hearths of the pitying farmers; but he only muttered, continually, "Poor Ralph is only a clodhopper; Miss Maria can't marry a clodhopper."

Maria, learning the terrible result of her trifling, and fearing to meet the wrath of her father, consented to fly to the city with the young man who had been her companion for the day. Little was afterwards known of her, in her native village. When, a few years afterwards, her father died, a lawyer from Pittsfield claimed his estate in her name, and it was sold. At a yet later day, there came a vague rumor that she was the wife of a great East India merchant, in New York, and lived surrounded by luxury. Mansions, servants, and equipages ministered to that vanity which in youth had demanded a sacrifice — alas, how much more costly! But no certain news came of her, and she never revisited the scenes of her youthful triumphs. Sometimes her name was there mentioned, and her story repeated, but year by year it grew less familiar, until now only a few decrepit dwellers in the past, love to recount it to a patient listener to such old tales, like myself. Certain I am, that, although some of my old friends have found the battle of life a hard combat, not one of them would exchange, for a moment, her bitter struggle with want and labor, for all the memory encumbered splendor of her ancient rival.

I lately visited the place where the cottage of Ralph once stood. It was entirely desolate. The lightnings had blasted even the feathery elm which used to overhang it; and it was bleached white, in the mountain storms. Of the garden, only a single rose-tree remained, growing rank with leaves and cankered blossoms. Was it too fanciful to believe that Nature had left them there — that tree and rose — memorials, the one of the blighted manliness of the lover, the other of the cankered prosperity of the coquette?

So ran the little story to which we listened, while the Ploughing Match of 1851 was passing. When it was ended, we proceeded to the hall, where the products of the orchard, the garden, the dairy, and the household manufactory, were collected. Here we found the most delicious fruits, — trophies won in hard combat with the Frost King, and carefully defended from the raids which Winter, with all his hosts, makes over the borders of Spring. Here, also, were great tubs of butter, and cheese, for which epicures, with gloating eyes, were zealously contending; and here were quilts, of every variety of quaint pattern and embroidery, resplendent with rich colors. Whatever Berkshire earth could be tortured into yielding; and whatever the skill and taste of Berkshire women could create, was there. Here, again, the matrimonial disposition of our people appeared; the handsomest quilts were labelled "wedding quilts;" the prettiest caps were "wedding night-caps," which, — alas, that this and that should come together! — were significantly pinned to some very handsome home-made cradles.

But, after all, the crowd of people was the thing best worth one's notice. Once among them, individuality was not to be dreamed of; it was the very height of presumption to consider your legs, arms, or even your head, as pertaining with any more propriety to yourself than to your neighbor; — all were merged in one commonweal, or better, in one common woe. And then if, by accident the mass was brought to a stand, the crash of bones, stay-lacings, watch crystals, and like frangibles, was really frightful. Nothing but a chivalric sense of duty could have induced me to go through the entire exhibition.

CHAPTER XVII.

WHAT THEY DO AT OTIS.

BY A LADY OF BOSTON.

WHEN we left you, at the Stockbridge House, there was a sort of half promise on my part, of sending you a weekly epistle, recording all my goings and comings, seeings and hearings. I wonder, now, how I ever came to agree to such a thing; it must have been the work of feelings softened by a parting "good bye!" to my ever delightful Cousin George. The truth is, it would take a whole fortnight of Otis to fill a sheet of lady like paper; but I'll tell you what I'll do, — writing a little, daily, I'll send you when we leave here the whole, "at one fell swoop."

I am sorry you did not come with us to this quiet little place, although you pretended to be ignorant of its very existence. Our gentlemen say, trout is very abundant in the streams, and pickerel in the lakes. They go out soon after breakfast, with guns and fishing rods, and usually come home laden with spoil.

But here I ought to give you some idea of our whereabout. I am now in Sister M.'s room, which is the best in the house, as is right and proper. Through three windows, all in a row, the bright afternoon sun is shining, making, if possible, more bright the red and orange of the carpet, the red and green of the bed curtains, and the yellow and green of the furniture generally, which, as you see, is all very gay. From these same windows may be seen the whole village. *The* street, with its two churches standing *vis-à-vis;* the school house, the lawyer's little white office and pretty dwelling house; the store just opposite, and a little lower down the post-office and blacksmith's shop; a number of neat cottages, and a few more aspiring mansions.

Just back of the church, on the hill side, is the village burying ground, close by the "Doctor's" house, as it should be.

From my window, at the back of the building, I see a narrow strip of meadow, through which winds a noisy little river, that somewhere beyond my ken "turns a mill," but whether for the sawing of boards or grinding of wheat, I cannot say. Then there is a small pond, covered with quantities of yellow lilies of a most odious odor. Over the pond is a bridge, crossing which you find a very pleasant walk, up the "east road." Wild flowers are there, in great variety and profusion. To me, accustomed to bouquets made to order, the freedom to pick and choose here is very delightful. Our hostess is astonished at the quantities of wild things which I bring home from my rambles; and, when I tell her that I think them very beautiful, she says, "Well, there's no accounting for people's tastes;" which is very true, indeed.

Around us rise the Berkshire hills, from which come down the most invigorating of breezes, — giving one the rosiest of cheeks and the heartiest of appetites.

Breakfast, with us, I assure you is anything but a mere ceremony; and the dinner bell is never an unwelcome sound.

Mr. F., the occupant of the pretty white office, and a very agreeable man, called last evening and planned several excursions; among others, one to "Otis Falls," which, he assures us, are well worth the visiting. I have made the acquaintance of Mr. F.'s two dogs, and think them both very interesting, in their way. There is another, seemingly ownerless, — a sort of canine loafer, following every one who encourages him, and wagging his tail in token of friendship, if you do but look at him. "Zach."— Zach. Taylor, they call him — is a large black and shaggy animal, whose escort is not always acceptable; but he seems to know that I am a visitor, and very rarely allows me to go out unattended.

Friday. — Yesterday, with a party from Lenox, we visited the Spring, which gives its name to the "Cold Spring Iron Works." We had a delightful ride of three miles, then a walk through a luxuriant turnip field, and a pretty piece of woods, when suddenly we found ourselves standing on the banks of a narrow river, with a high, steep hill rising close behind us, covered with silver birch. Half way up the hill-side a rude seat had been placed among the trees, and just below it is the beautiful spring, of whose clear, cold waters every visitor is expected to drink, and afterwards to lave his hands in its pebbly basin. Around we found some gorgeous cardinal flowers, foxgloves, and many other flowers of unknown names, but with bloom and fragrance not less sweet for that. We are happy and willing to testify that a prettier spot is not to be found in Berkshire, nor colder water this side of Greenland.

On our return, we looked into the "Forge," and saw men hammering iron, as warm as if there were no "cold spring" within a hundred miles of them. Now, Cousin, will you ever say again that you never heard of such a place as Otis?

John has just come in with a pair of gloves, which he "inclines to think need mending;" and I, like a pattern cousin, am going to sew up the rips. So adieu!

Monday. — On Saturday we went to *the* Falls. The morning seemed specially made for our purpose, and we started in the highest spirits. All the way the road kept close by the little river, which here meets us at every turn. Fine trees grew on either side of the road, often intermingling their branches overhead, and forming a sort of triumphal arch, "long drawn out." The waters sparkled and gleamed up among the leaves; the wild flowers — the laurel most beautiful of all — were in full bloom; the birds sang sweetly; "in short," as Mr. Micawber would say, "everything was *color de rose.*" Even Miss T. forgot that "her sun bonnet made her look like a fright," and sat in perfect contentment.

We were almost sorry when we came to the little village of Cold Spring, three miles from the village of Otis, where we dined, and then laid our course for the Falls. Here we separated from Mr. and Mrs. B., who went round in the carriage, while we preferred climbing up and over a very steep mountain, although it certainly did not present a very attractive appearance.

15*

Almost destitute of trees, and covered with short, dry grass, so slippery was the way that we could hardly keep our feet. But we were desirous of doing something "out of the common," so, with a boy for a guide, we commenced our ascent.

There was something entirely amusing in slipping down and being pulled up, in catching hold of alder bushes for support, taking in breath to last another trial, and then making it. When we did come to a tree, that was a special blessing. Almost at the summit we met with one — a very ancient broad-branched apple tree, in whose shade we stayed a quarter of an hour. It had fruit, too, — Mr. T.'s cane soon brought us a specimen, and he insisted upon our eating it. Miss T. made the attempt, and declared it entirely impossible; but when John, with his most engaging smile, besought her to eat half of his, she had not the heart to refuse. Her brother muttered something about Eve and the serpent. Yes; that was a pleasant quarter of an hour under the old apple tree; while Miss T. took the opportunity to alter the strings of her bonnet, Cousin Jack talked an immense deal of poetry, and Mr. T. decorated my hat with leaves from the old apple tree, vastly admiring his own handiwork.

The remainder of the ascent was soon climbed; we caught glimpses of houses, and saw before us an open road; stone fences now came to be very frequent, and we became proficients in climbing them. Crossing the road we entered a rough-looking piece of woodland, where we heard the roar of the water. It grew louder and louder, as we descended into the wildest looking ravine you can imagine. Rude steps were made to assist our descent, and we soon found ourselves in the very presence of the Fall.

M. and her spouse were there, ready to "do the honors," and seemingly on very intimate terms with Majesty. Description is not my forte, or you should have all the characteristics of the cataract, — its length, breadth, quantity of water, and all that. You must now be content to know that they are beautiful and sublime, — beautiful enough to call forth all your "Oh's" and "Ah's" of delight; grand enough to fill you with admiration, without making you feel miserably insignificant in comparison, — a combination of qualities much to be desired.

High rocks rise perpendicularly on either side, and as far as the eye can reach, the river goes roaring and foaming between them, in a very boisterous style. I cannot think that, in all its course, it ever becomes a quiet, orderly, well-behaved stream. I ought to speak a good word for the Falls, for they got up a rainbow for our especial benefit, — and Niagara could have done no more. We stayed until the last moment possible; but when we set our faces homeward, we were quite willing to abandon pedestrianism. Very tired indeed we were, and yet even more delighted with our day's excursion. Two days only remain, of our visit here, so that you will not get a very long Otis journal.

Tuesday. — This morning I strolled into the burial ground, and it struck me as the most uninviting place in the village. I wondered if the dead could sleep well beneath its sod. Nothing in the world could tempt me to be buried there; I could never rest quietly. I am sure no ghost of taste would think a moment of walking in such a jungle of thistles and blackberry bushes.

At Mount Auburn, where Nature and Art are both in such perfection, my thoughts are occupied with the beautiful sculpture, the rare trees, the lovely walks to the exclusion of its silent inhabitants; but here, the absence of every attraction compelled me to think of the Unseen, — and, leaning against the rude fence, I mused long, if not deeply, on that great mystery — Death. [Godfrey thinks this latter much the more proper and profitable subject for his fair friend's contemplation, and hopes it may occur again.] Do not suppose I am going to trouble you with my speculations; they were too vague, if I had the wish to do so.

It was curious how strongly came back to me my old childish feelings, when, a little girl, I used to have the gloomiest thoughts of being buried. The idea of being carried *out* from my home, and left all alone in the grave-yard, was very, very dreadful; many bitter tears have I shed over my own obsequies. I envied the mummies which I read of in my First Class Book,

> "Who walked about
> In Thebe's streets, three thousand years ago,"

and yet were standing up, if not walking. It seemed to me that I should not fear death so much, if I could be made like one of them, and placed in Sister Mary's closet, which she visited two or three times every day. Once I remember to have expressed a wish of the kind, but the look of horror with which my proposition was received, quite precluded any hope of such an indulgence being granted.

Even now I have something left of that old feeling; my spirit still loves its earthly tenement, as one does the house in which he was born, and has passed many years of joy and sorrow. I love to believe that my own body will be raised a heavenly one, for I know my spirit would not feel quite at home in an angel's form.

I was still in deep thought, when I heard a rushing sound, and saw the blackberry bushes and thistles in violent commotion. I was at first in great alarm, not knowing what wild beast might have made his lair in these savage haunts; and I was not a little relieved when I saw my self-constituted esquire, "Zach," making his way towards me. He seemed perfectly wild with joy, at my unusually cordial reception, and accompanied me home without any refusals on my part.

This is my last day in Otis. With the hope of your presence in Boston the coming Winter, and of many letters in the meantime, I subscribe myself

Your affectionate

COUSIN WINIFRED.

CHAPTER XVIII.

PITTSFIELD YOUNG LADIES' INSTITUTE.

It is like a picture in an old story book about France *la belle*, with arching trees in front, a temple and château in the back-ground, and maidens and peasant-girls in all — is the scene at our Young Ladies' Institute, of a pleasant Summer twilight. All its light hearted inmates are out in full glee, with circling games and ringing laughter, — the truest children of health, content, and innocence.

But all are not in the giddy group; some have separated from it, and, in couples, with arms affectionately intertwined, are slowly walking down the long paths, pouring into each other's ears the precious secrets of maiden confidence, — all the hopes, the dreams, the fears which can find a lodging place in pure hearts. Very precious are those hopes and fears; although neither may ever be realized, yet shall they be a part of life and a part of the woman in all her future. In this life of ours, we pile dream upon dream, effort upon disappointed effort, until the apparent fruitlessness attains to some sort of fruition and reality. There are few things in poetry more beautifully and truthfully said, than these lines of Henry Taylor: —

"The tree
Sucks kindlier nature from a soil enriched
By its own fallen leaves; and Man is made
In heart and spirit from deciduous hopes,
And things which seem to perish."

Under the vine shaded bowers, or by the sparkling fountain, sits here and there a solitary maiden, with thoughts, perhaps, far away in a happy home; striving to bring to her fancy the family group as it is in the old homestead at the pleasant close of day. She may well be pardoned if, even in this pleasant home of learning, she steals a little while from young companionship, to let the warm but not bitter tears run freely down her cheeks. She will soon rejoin the merry circle, not the least merry there.

This Institute is becoming a marvel of beautiful completeness. Nothing in our village is more attractive to a stranger's eye than its broad ornamental grounds, with their winding walks and drives; their bowers, trees, hedges, and shrubbery, in the centre of which are grouped the chapel, gymnasium, and dormitories.

The chapel is a most chaste and elegant structure, modelled accurately after that portico of the Erecthion at Athens, dedicated to Minerva Polias. Classic antiquarians tell us that in this portico was the sacred olive tree, created by Minerva at the foundation of the citadel, and that here also was kept, guarded by dragons, the Erichthonian image of the same goddess — the Athenian Palladium. Perhaps there may be a bit of pedantry in it, but one cannot help suggesting that in our temple also is kept a Palladium, whose safety is quite as essential to the well being of the State as that of old was fabled to be to the welfare of Athens

— the education, virtue, and piety of American women. I am afraid, now, some wicked youth will pursue the simile farther, and add that our modern Palladium, like the ancient, is guarded by dragons; to which I can only reply, that I know no more amiable and pleasant people than these same dragons, at least when off duty; I cannot answer for other times.

This chapel is as chaste and beautiful within, as it is without. On either side a broad passage way, paved with blue and white marble mosaic, are arranged convenient rooms for classes, cabinets, and like purposes. From this we ascend, by a broad and easy flight of stairs, to a large, airy hall, handsomely frescoed, and perfectly ventilated. The furniture of this room is very rich and costly, especially the magnificent organ and piano, — which, under the hands of M. Trenckler and his pupils, are made to speak to the very soul. Few of the musical lions, who of late have set the country wild, have half the genius of this gentleman, who, with the modesty of a master, shrinks from the public gaze. In this chapel hall the school daily assembles. Here, also, are held the Semi-Annual Examinations and the Musical Soirèes. I make it a point to attend these examinations, both as a matter of pleasure and profit. Poetry and philosophy, believe me, sound none the less pleasantly when they come from rosy lips; no, nor any the less truthfully. Why! I have seen an eminent D.D. enter into a discussion with a witty Miss, on one of these occasions, and the worthy divine did not come off triumphant.

But, if I begin on this theme, there is no telling where I may end; and besides, I should trench on the province of the honorables, the reverends, and the venerables, who will form the next examining committee. What puzzles me, is how masculine vanity ever grew so enormously as to fancy its possessor had more sconce than womankind. It is strange, again, how the idea ever obtained, that learning was a sort of compensating perquisite for ugly women. One who attends an Institute Examination would say that beauty and brains go as naturally together as strawberries and cream.

To tell of the delicious musical réunions would lead me more widely astray than the dryer details of an examination, — inasmuch as I love music as cordially as I detest mathematics; yet I suppose the latter must in some way be digested. Indeed, I am told some young ladies "dote on them." It is odd to hear silver toned voices rattling off plus and minus, sines and cosines, arcs, segments and tangents, with as much zest as "Ah, non giunge," or "Oft in the stilly night." But, seriously, one thing speaks well for the balance of education here, and that is, — that the voice which most clearly elucidates a problem of Euclid in the morning, shall also most accurately analyze a passage of Milton in the afternoon, and perhaps charm you with some sweet strain of music in the evening. Of course this nice balance is only found in those who, commencing early, persevere through a complete course of study. But I am running on as I said I would not.

The most novel of the provisions which Mr. Tyler has made, for the benefit of his pupils, is the splendid Gymnasium — I believe the most costly and complete thing of its kind, connected with any institution of learning, in the country. It is a very large and finely proportioned building, of two stories, — the lower divided into musical and painting rooms, and the like. The upper forms a magnificent hall, eighty feet long by fifty wide, with a graceful arch in the centre, supported by two fine colonnades of Ionic pillars. From this arch are suspended ropes, swings, and a variety of calisthenic apparatus, — which can easily be placed aside, leaving the broad area open, for the enjoyment of the freest hilarity.

On either side this open space, within the colonnades, are two bowling alleys — four in all — which entice the pupils to continual practice of that most genial and healthful exercise. The value of systematic exercise has been the constant theme of teachers for years. The rewards which its practice would ensure, and the sad punishment for its neglect, used to be painted to us at school, in glowing colors, — whose truthfulness too many of us can now painfully recognise.

I do not know that we then believed them false, but the want of those facilities which Mr. Tyler has so amply supplied, were a sore temptation to brave the danger. Heretofore, the attempt to supply this deficiency has been wofully inefficient. Although it is essential that the place of exercise should be well ventilated, and of attractive appearance, yet whenever a room has been provided, it has generally been some close, rough, cobwebed hall — an unsightly place, without beauty or fitness. It is to be hoped that the example of Mr. Tyler, in reforming this matter altogether, will be appreciated and followed.

Leaving this hall, we ascended, by several flights of stairs, to the cupola, where we were astonished at the beautiful bird's-eye view of the valley which presented itself. I think nothing of the kind in Pittsfield can surpass it.

The "Institute" is not the only seminary of the kind in our village. The pleasant family school of Miss Wells, although without the costly and luxurious appliances of the Institute, is hardly, if at all, inferior to it in successful teaching. I have never listened to the public exhibition of scholarship at this school, but its graduates are possessed of accomplishments which any institute might be proud to have bestowed. Nothing can be more pleasant than the "Musical Soirées" at this school. The unaffected style and splendid execution of Mr. Crossman, and his pupils, is beyond praise, in this age of rampant bravuras and crashing symphonies.

CHAPTER XIX.

LANESBORO'.—HILLS AND VALLEYS.

NESTLED closest in the bosom of our hills lies the little village of Lanesboro'—the very fondling of Nature. Thither turns never the good mother her wrinkled front; near pressing as the mountains clasp the narrow valley, you must not look among them for frowning precipices, or earthquake rifted chasms. High into the air their summits press, but not in jagged peaks—only with the full, round swelling of loving breasts, upon which you may repose, if you will, in the gentlest of Summer reveries.

There is one eminence—in patriotic gratitude they call it Constitution Hill—with such a winsome, neighborly look to it, that in our streets, miles away, it seems near as your own garden. If you have in you any yearnings at all after beauty, I am sure you cannot look upon, and not be irresistibly drawn to it, to be lifted up gently and humanly, above the baser things of earth. Lying under its druidical oaks, or seated, farther up, upon a pearl-white quartz rock, in the shade of a whispering birch, you will see below you groves and farms, and broad, fresh meadows, with laughing lakes and winding rivulets,—like silver embroidery on the green banner of Erin.

Many fair villages, as well, will dot the scene, whose names — if you do not know — I hope you will never ask, but be content to remember, that under each roof of them all, human lives are wearing themselves out. Then let your own heart interpret for you what the overlooking woods whisper. If you know well the story of one hearth-stone, think what a thrilling tale it is; and if, in your reveries upon the hill-tops you multiply that marvellous but common story into the thousand dwellings of the valley, the resultant mass shall be greater than the mountains which encompass it.

I could point you to an antique mansion — a grey spot it appears in the far distance, with no overhanging cloud to distinguish it — at whose story I am deeply moved, as often as I look upon it. The splendors and the shadows, which have by turns darkened and illumined its chambers, pass and repass in spectral reiteration, over my spirit. Whether I will or not, come the ghosts of fleeting joys, irradicable sorrows; the loftiness of human pride and lowliness of pride's abasement, which have passed and left no record there; and yet that grey old homestead is no accursed roof, devoted to misery from its foundation, but one even such as its fellows are. Ah! if we could look within the seemly exterior of any home, — if we could penetrate the heart's chambers of any man, what might not meet us there? Those glowing windows which gleam so cheerily on our evening path, by what funereal torches may they not be lighted? Those radiant faces which meet us smilingly in our noonday walk, by what infernal passions may they not be driven on? So under the green and smiling earth lie pent the hidden fires, and help the genial sun to quicken the blossom and ripen the fruit.

This Constitution Hill must be a great promoter of reverie. I have a friend — a bachelor friend — who, no sooner is he seated upon it, than off he goes dreaming over the whole valley, in a very Marvel-ous way. I do not believe there is a dwelling in sight, from Greylock to Taghconic, that he has not, at sometime, made himself *pater familias* in it. Bring him up hither, and his respect for the Tenth Commandment vanishes like the mist of the valley. Another friend of mine — an artist — never looks down from hence, but — presto! change! — the hard work of a century all gone, and the red Indian come back again, with wild wood and wigwam, council fire and hunting ground. So you, if you come within the charmed circle of our hills' shaven crown, may, perchance, work some wonderful phantasmagoric changes.

I do not know how it all comes about. Perhaps some good genius has cast a spell upon the spot — a mode of solving such difficulties to which I confess myself prone, being naturally of a superstitious as well as lymphatic turn of mind.

It may be only another fancy of mine, but the leaves here seem to have a perfection of beauty not attained elsewhere. Nature's work is finished with more care; the curves are cut with a more accurate grace, and the green more faithfully laid on. In the Fall, too, the rich enamellings are done with greater depth of coloring, and without shrivelling up the work in the process, as the careless elves are very apt to do in other groves. The specimens of their workmanship which I have seen here, were perfect gems in their way. You shall not desire to see a more gorgeous sight than Constitution Hill in October.

Just on the western declivity is a good sized cavern, which, a witty lady thinks, may be the home of these elfin workmen; but, in spite of the high authority, I must doubt; such underground tenements are more fit dwelling places for bears, wolves, and such like ugly gnomes, than for any gentle spirits whatever. No, ours are

> "Some gay creatures of the elements,
> Who in the colors of the rainbow live
> And play 'i the plighted clouds."

Descending from the hill, you may wander up the stream which flows at its base. If a follower of the "gentle craft of angling," you will not neglect to lie awhile where some thick-leaved maple overshadows a deep pool, where you may drop your line with the reasonable hope of bringing to shore a dozen fine fish — perhaps even the "Hermit Trout" himself, who is believed to haunt these pools, and only dimple the shallows in the pale moonlight; — a wary old fellow he,

> "Too shrewd
> To be by a wading boy pulled out!"

Indeed, this is a stream which would have charmed old Izaak — the very counterpart of his own transparent Ichen. But I trust you are no patron of his treacherous sport. You were better to sit on some warm bank of green sward, or dangling your feet over some rustic bridge, to watch the smoothly gliding current, and

"The shadows of sun-gilt ripples
On the pebbly bed of a brook."

There is no wine, or oil of gladness, which has such a balm for the wounded spirit as the soft murmurs of a rural brooklet.

Wandering on, you may, if you are fortunate as I have been, sometimes catch a glimpse into dream-land, — like a vignette to an old romance, of a youth seated under a spreading elm, with a guitar in his hand and a maiden by his side. When I was a citizen I used to think such things confined to poetry and Spain; but here, in the quiet days of Summer, things often occur which convince one of the truth of Hood's remark, that "it is dangerous to swear to the truth or falsehood of a romance, even of one's own making."

On a gentle hillock, by whose side the stream flows in deep willow shade, is the village grave-yard. Do not fail to enter it. Among its thick, clustering monuments you can linger with best profit, undisturbed by quaintly ludicrous epitaphs, or monstrous heraldries of death. The touching inscriptions on the simple marbles bespeak alike the chastened spirit and the cultivated mind. What wild woe — paternal, filial, fraternal, and conjugal — this narrow spot has witnessed, I shrink from recalling. The marble bears record only of the subdued grief and the christian hope; the story of the early woe, when the one joy of life perished, — when "the young green bole was marked for fellage," is not told to the stranger's eye, and is sacred from the stranger's pen. Yet to that stranger is the place deeply consecrated; how holy, then, to those whose best of earth is mingled with its dust. I am here often reminded of a beautiful thought of Richter. "The ancients had it that not even the ashes of the dead should be embarked with the living, for fear of the storm which would be sure to follow. We have learned better, and know that, to be accompanied on the voyage of life by the memory of the dead, brings calm, and not storm; he who always feels one loss, will be less accessible to new sorrow."

The Old Worshipper.

In this grave-yard I once witnessed a scene, so touching and solemn, and yet so far removed from any agony of woe, that to speak of it can open anew no half healed wound. It was one of those occasions when the sorrows of earth are so gloriously transmuted into the joys of Heaven, that we, who remain "of the earth, earthy," look upon the transfiguration in far off wonder; while Philosophy strives in vain to characterize emotions, in which the consoler, Christ, enables the mourner to mingle — as in His own mysterious nature — so much of human sorrow with so much of Divine confidence.

Not far from the village grave-yard is the church, — a modest gothic structure, built of the grey stone of the county. This was once, for many months, my own place of worship; and still, on a pleasant Sabbath morning, I love to stroll to it. The bracing walk of some half dozen miles, through a delightful country, is no unworthy preparation for the devotions of the sanctuary; and, through the day, the voices of woods and waters seem to mingle with the deep responses of the congregation. Nature, with her thousand voices, joins in the jubilant chorus, and in subdued tones echoes the supplications of the solemn litany.

The first morning upon which I entered this church I was struck with the venerable figure of an old man, who sat in front of me, completely absorbed in worship. Never had my ideal of Christian devotion been so completely filled; no painter could have desired a finer model. His whole soul seemed informed and penetrated with the spirit of the liturgy, in whose eloquent words he poured forth his soul to GOD.

His veteran form was tall and martial in its bearing; in the deep lines of his countenance you could not mistake the characters of strong intellect, self respect, and unbending firmness of purpose. You would say he was one not likely to yield much obsequious homage to his fellow man; but here, in the presence of Jehovah, his whole bearing was conformed to the most lowly, yet manly, humility. Nothing could be more impressive than the earnest tones with which he joined in the services of the church.

Sabbath after Sabbath my eye sought and found him — the most noticeable figure in the room — until one Summer's day, when I entered, the people were waiting, in that hush of expectation which in a country congregation tells one that a funeral is about to take place. On my way to the church I had lingered a few moments, as was my wont, in the grave-yard, — and had found an open grave in the lot of the venerable worshipper. I now looked to his pew; it was vacant; and I at once guessed that it was he who was about to enter the sacred portals for the last time. But it was not so; a whisper from a neighbor informed me that it was the wife of the old man who was no more — the wife of his youth.

Presently, as the procession entered, I saw the widowed husband following close behind the coffin, his head a little bent, as if to approach nearer the form of the sleeper, and his voice a little more tremulous than usual, as he joined in the Scripture appointed to be then read.

The coffin was laid before the altar, and the old man took his seat, with that forced calmness where the quivering lip shows the struggle hardly yet over, and the victory only half won.

As the sublime promises of future reunion were read; as the sympathizing tones of consolation fell from the lips of the preacher, I thought the few remaining clouds vanished from the aged face, and a perfect serenity overspread it. When the sermon was ended, with an aspect almost cheerful, he rose up, to follow to her burial place all that remained on earth of her, with whom, for more than fifty years, he had walked, in sunshine and storm. What emotions were at work within, none could read; — the fixed eye, the firm set lip, revealed nothing, — the prying eye of curiosity, the anxious gaze of friendship, returned alike, baffled. And yet, with what overwhelming power must the busy memory of that lonely old man have brought back the thick crowding events of half a century, from the first thrilling meeting to this last brief parting! It is such moments which must disclose most vividly to the mind of Eld what this life is which passeth like a dream.

Such might have been the retrospect of the mourner of three score years and ten, as he took his few brief steps from the temple to the tomb; — or, perchance his better spirit reached forward to a glorious meeting in that home to which sorrow and parting can never come.

The coffin was lowered to its place; — the people gathered around. The pastor began that beautiful service, in which the church commits earth to its kindred earth, and proclaims the spirit returned to the GOD who gave it. There, at the clergyman's side, stood the tall and veteran form of the mourner, his thin grey hairs streaming in the mountain wind, as he repeated, firmly, the proper responses. For a while he looked steadfastly down into the grave, — but as the pastor read: — "And the corruptible bodies of those who sleep in Him shall be changed and made like unto His own glorious body," the depressed eyes were raised to Heaven with an expression of most triumphant and joyous hope. The struggle was over. The grave had lost its sting; — "Death was swallowed up in victory." It was a spectacle most touching and sublime.

Yet a few moments, and the grave was closed; the people separated to their homes, — and the mourner, likewise, departed to his, — but for not long. He was soon missed from his accustomed seat in the sanctuary. With the fall of the leaf, he went down into the grave, — and the grass which in the Spring started upon his wife's mound, waved over two.

There is another and older graveyard in the town, white with its multitude of marble testimonials. Here there used to be a tomb, carved with masonic symbols, and having a heavy iron knocker on its door. Here, often at midnight, — whether the still moon shed her pale light on the ghastly tombstones, or the dark and howling tempest was on, — a crazed woman used to enter the grave encumbered ground, and strike such a peal on the ringing iron that the sleepers in the near dwellings started trembling from their slumbers. There is something terribly significant to me in that gloomy visitation of the tomb. What earnestness of agonized longing for their repose, may have impelled that wild nocturnal summons to the dead. "Wake! wake! ye peaceful dwellers in the tomb," perhaps that weary, brainsick woman said; "open your dark portals and give me rest beside ye; wake! — the living turn from me, and do you also spurn me? — me, who shudder not at any loathsomeness of yours?"

But cheerier thoughts for the cheerful light of Summer, — and, passing the mildewed realms of death, do you hie away to some beautiful hill, — Platt's, Prospect, St. Luke's, or the "Noppet;" or to some fair valley, — whither I may not stay to accompany you, — and so, farewell!

CHAPTER XX.

GRANULAR QUARTZ. — SILICIOUS SAND BEDS.

NOT the least curious geological formation in America is that of the granular quartz beds, among the Berkshire hills. Much fierce warfare has been waged, among the irascible sons of science, as to how and when they came where we now find them; whether they form part of the regular strata, or are interlopers in the family of old Hoosac. If I rightly understood him, I once heard a dignified savan distinctly charge them with being no better than changelings; and the whole learned conclave agreed, that Nature must have brought them forth in a gypsy sort of a way, not very creditable to her.

I do not know that I could reconcile the differences of the doctors — even if I understood them — but this much a love of justice compels me to say, that, having visited these rocks in their homes, from Vermont to Connecticut, I have always found them lying among Nature's other children as peaceably as need be, — although I must confess that their neighbors often bear traces of fiery times and a good deal of turmoil, when the quartz first came among them, perhaps with some unseemly ardor and abruptness; but for immaculate purity, the wide world cannot show their equal.

Without metaphor, the beds of granular quartz scattered along the Hoosac Mountains, afford, in some of their localities, the most precious and beautiful silicious sand for the glass manufacturer, which the world has ever known.

For thousands of years this has been considered one of the most rare and valuable minerals. Tacitus tells us that it was found on the banks of the river Belus, near Mt. Carmel, and used by the Phœnicians, three thousand years ago. Nitre, he adds, was found naturally combined with it; and, although the shore was small, the supply was considered inexhaustible. At the time of the advent of Our Saviour, vessels were annually dispatched to this locality to bring the sand to Rome, where extensive glass manufactories had been established. Then, and long afterwards, Mt. Carmel was supposed to be the only locality of glass-making sand in the world. Excellent beds have since been opened, in various parts of Europe; but in England, until within a century, ground flints were used exclusively in the manufactories; whence the name, "Flint Glass." Lynne sand was afterwards found to be nearly pure silicious matter, and that was substituted. More lately I understand a still better article has been discovered at Alum Bay, in the Isle of Wight.

A curious item in the statistics of English glass making accounts for the exceeding ugliness of junk bottles. It seems that the British excise laws forbid the use of any better material in their manufacture than the sand from the river bottom, lest the revenue might be defrauded by the use of the glass for purposes where one which pays a higher tax is now employed.

Great quantities of sand are taken, for this purpose, from the bed of the Thames, opposite Woolwich — from which comes the name of "Woolwich Glass."

Until within a few years, the American glass houses have been supplied with silicious material from the banks of the Delaware and Mississippi, and from a locality near Pittsburgh, Penn. But about the year 1847, the sand beds of Berkshire attracted the attention of Mr. SAMUEL SMITH, of Boston, by whom their product was introduced to the notice of nearly, if not quite, all the manufacturers of New York and New England, as well as to some of those in more distant places. The glass houses of the northern States, except Pennsylvania, are now supplied almost exclusively from these beds.

The existence of an excellent silicious sand in Berkshire, has been long known. Indeed, in 1814 glass houses were established in Cheshire and Chester, in this county. But the difficulty of transportation over the hills was then very great, and, together with the influx of foreign goods, consequent upon the return of Peace, rendered these enterprises unprofitable, and both were very shortly abandoned. From that time until the year 1848, the beds were neglected almost entirely — being worked, I believe, only for the use of marble sawyers, and for the glass works at Sand Lake, in New York.

In this latter year, a bed in the eastern part of the town of Lanesboro' (known now as the "Old Berkshire Bed") was opened, to supply the markets. This still remains the most valuable bed, and is, I think, the only one now worked. I may as well attempt some description of it, as it appeared on a recent visit.

At a distance of some six miles from Pittsfield we came to a bye road, leading circuitously across the fields to the east. One of the windings of this cross road brought us suddenly upon what — if it had not been July, I should have taken for an immense snow drift. It was a pile of silicious sand, containing something like three thousand tons. It was white and fine as the purest snow that is driven over our mountains. The imagination can conceive of nothing more brilliantly white than this mass, glittering in a July's sun. Strangers exhaust their rhetoric in their attempts at comparison. — The driven snow, salt, loaf sugar, the silver fleece, the fleecy cloud, are all impressed into service. One *very* young gentleman likened it to his lady's bosom!

They tell a story of one Mr. R., of Lanesboro', whose good lady had a box of this sand placed upon the shelf, close by a similar box of salt; but the two getting somehow transposed, Mr. R. gave the sand to his horses, for salt, for some days, before he discovered his mistake, — for the beasts made no mention of it, although undoubtedly they had it on their tongues.

I can vouch for the truth of this story; but the proverbial honesty of gentlemen of that trade forbids me to credit the slanderous report that the grocers use the same article to give weight to their sugars.

The bank of sand which I described, lay a dazzling mass in the sunshine. Beyond it a pit some eighty feet deep, and of large area, was dug into the mountain. The west side is open to the road, for drainage and transportation. The other sides, or walls, as they are technically called, are of solid granular quartz, softened in some parts to sand, by the action of water and air, and here and there intersected by a vein of fire clay. Several feet of superincumbent soil rest upon it.

Across the top of the pit a wooden viaduct leads a mountain brook to a series of wooden vats, with strainers of wire gauze at the lower end of each. These are filled with sand, — passing in succession from one to the other, — and the water is filtered through them, carrying with it whatever impurities may be present. When this purification is completed, the sand is thrown out to dry in the sun; but a great deal of moisture remains, which cannot be thus evaporated, and accordingly it is taken to the drying house, which stands on the main road nearly at the point where the bye road leaves it. Here it is placed in huge pans, made of closely riveted boiler iron, under which a brisk fire is kept up until no moisture remains. It is then packed in barrels and sent to market.

Other beds of this mineral have been wrought, but none are so well worthy of a visit as the one I have described.

CHAPTER XXI.

MONUMENT MOUNTAIN. — ICY GLEN. — STOCKBRIDGE BOWL. — THE MURDERED TRAVELLER'S GLEN.

So much has been written about the fair old town of Stockbridge, that the tourist finds almost every rood upon which he there treads, already storied ground. Seldom does genius owe so much to its dwelling place, and yet more rarely is the debt so richly paid. "What is writ is writ," and it is hardly worth a common man's while to celebrate anew scenes which have received their fame at the hands of Bryant and Miss Sedgwick. Yet it is some compensation that the dry details, the skeleton topography of places so consecrated, are read with interest. In such topographical style let us run briefly over the regions about "Old" Stockbridge.

Our first visit was to Monument Mountain, which, although within the limits of Great Barrington, is in the immediate neighborhood of Stockbridge village. No description of it can be more perfect than that given by Bryant.

"There is a precipice,
Which seems a fragment of some mighty wall,
Built by the hand which fashioned the old world
To separate its nations, and thrown down
When the flood drowned them. To the north a path

Conducts you up the narrow battlement.
Steep is the western side, shaggy and wild
With mossy trees and pinnacles of flint,
And many a hanging crag. But to the east,
Sheer to the vale go down the bare old cliffs,—
Huge pillars that in middle Heaven uprear
Their weather-beaten capitals, here dark
With the thick moss of centuries, and there
Of chalky whiteness, where the thunderbolt
Hath splintered them."

When I used, in school days, to steal the moments due to dryer studies to read in the old "National Reader," of Monument Mountain and

"Its sad tradition of unhappy love
And sorrows borne and ended long ago,"

I little dreamed that I should ever stand at its base, in the glorious light of a Berkshire morning, to compute the marketable value of "the bare old cliffs." Thank Heaven they are, after all, not of a nature to tempt the avarice of man!

The precipice rises five hundred feet, perpendicularly — or a little beetling at the top; it is slightly curved inward, and gradually decreases in height, towards the south. At the bottom are heaped up a great mass of angular fragments, which have from time to time fallen from it; and a detached pinnacle stands at a little distance, which is called "The Pulpit Rock," but reminded me more of a ruined and isolated tower of some old baronial castle. Cliff and fragment, and isolated crag, are formed of a compact granular quartz, — the same substance which, farther north, when disintegrated by some natural process, forms the silicious sand of commerce.

The precipice extends north to about the middle of the Mountain, where it disappears, and the geological character of the rock is changed to that of mica slate. At the juncture rises the path by which you reach the summit; and here I found some pretty crystals of black tourmaline. Climbing the ascent, which is just difficult enough to give a zest to it, I bent my head dizzily over the abyss.

> "It *is* a fearful thing
> To stand upon the beetling verge and see
> Where storm and lightning, from that grey old wall
> Have tumbled down vast blocks, and at the base
> Dashed them in fragments; and to lay thine ear
> Over the dizzy depth, and hear the sound
> Of winds, that struggle with the woods below,
> Come up like murmurs."

The pile of loose stones, which gave name to the mountain, was destroyed in wantonness or idle curiosity, many years ago. I have been told, however, that the pious contributions of visitors — who adopted the Indian custom of casting a stone upon it, as they passed — have quite restored it. I did not see it, for my guide said there was no monument now, nor ever had been. In fact, he had very little respect for the romancings of "Kate Sedgwick and Cullen Bryant," as he somewhat familiarly styled these distinguished personages. The story of the Indian maiden he considered to be a sheer sham — with no foundation in fact; or even worse, with one so detestably unpoetic I will not mar your pleasure in the scene by recording it.

From Monument Mountain we drove to ICY GLEN. I had long impatiently anticipated a visit to this celebrated ravine, and fancied often to myself what sort of a place it might be. I cannot say much for the accuracy of my preconceived notions. It is a deep and narrow gorge, cumbered with enormous boulders and fallen trees, slippery and mossy, piled up irregularly, so as to leave great cavernous recesses beneath, and to give passage to a brawling stream among them. There are, in Berkshire, few or no places of a more romantic wildness. When, after stumbling and tumbling, climbing and sliding, over and under these Devil's playthings of rocks, one emerges just at sunset upon the mellow rural scene without, he is prepared to welcome ecstatically the smiling landscape.

Within the glen there is sometimes a scene which must be grandly picturesque, — when on a moonless and, perhaps starless night, some hundred people in fantastic costumes, with flaming torches and pealing music, pass through the ravine, in such broken procession as over that crazy pathway they can. How the red glare of the torch-light must flash from the rugged surface of the rocks to the fair faces of the ladies, — never so fair as in such fitful light. How the mingling music, and laughter, and shouts must reëcho in a thousand Babel discordances, till the whole glen is mazed.

Thence by a charming road to the STOCKBRIDGE BOWL, the most famous, — by many thought the most beautiful of our mountain lakelets. Celebrated by the loving pens of Miss Sedgwick and Mrs. Sigourney, it has associations which our more northern lakes cannot boast. It is a graceful and gentle sheet of water, encircled by a fine rural country.

"The Stockbridge bowl! Hast ever seen
How sweetly pure and bright,

Its foot of stone, and rim of green
Attract the traveller's sight?—
High set among the breezy hills,
Where spotless marble glows,
It takes the tribute of the rills
Distilled from mountain snows."

SIGOURNEY.

To the other attractions of this lake, at the time of our visit, was added, that upon its banks then lived Nathaniel Hawthorne. It was no small thing to breathe for a while the same air with that marvellous genius. The mountain lake should record that brief acquaintance as its first honor. By the bye, I am told Mr. Hawthorne honored the mountain and the lake with far more of his attention than he bestowed upon his neighbors. I believe Herman Mellville and G. P. R. James were among his friends; but for the most part he is said to have lived in great seclusion. One is not much surprised to learn that the creator of Hester Prynne and little Pearl, Zenobia, and the Pynchons, does not find his highest pleasure in the chit-chat of fashionable or even of literary coteries. Nor should it surprise us if a touch of melancholy, or even seeming moroseness, tinges his manner. The knowledge of the soul's anatomist is that which "by suffering entereth."

The scene of Bryant's ballad of "The Murdered Traveller," is on the road between the villages of Old and West Stockbridge. The following is the poet's account of it, in his note: "Some years since, in the month of May, the remains of a human being, partly devoured by wild beasts, were found in a woody ravine near a solitary road between the mountains, west of Stockbridge. It was supposed that the person came to his death by violence, but no traces could be discovered of his murderers. It was only recollected that one evening in the previous Winter, a traveller had stopped at an inn in West Stockbridge; that he had enquired the way to Stockbridge, and that, in paying the landlord for something which he had ordered, it appeared he had a considerable sum of money in his possession.

"Two ill-looking men were present, and went out about the time the traveller proceeded on his journey. During the Winter, also, two ill-dressed men, but plentifully supplied with money, had lingered awhile about the village. Several years afterwards, a criminal, about to be executed in Canada, for a capital offence, confessed that he had been concerned in murdering a traveller for his money, near Stockbridge. Nothing was ever known of the name or residence of the person murdered."

Such is the foundation of Bryant's simple and touching ballad.

There are other beautiful and storied scenes about this most beautiful town, but space begins to fail me, and I must pass them. Green River, and the Sacrifice Rock, are left until another day.

NOTE. I regret deeply that I am unable to give a chapter here on Great Barrington — one of our most lovely towns — once the residence of Bryant; and also upon Bash Bish — one of our most picturesque localities. But a gentleman of Great Barrington, who had promised to contribute such a chapter, was compelled, by a pressure of business, to disappoint me, when it was too late to remedy the matter.

CHAPTER XXII.

WAHCONAH'S FALLS, AND A TRADITION ABOUT THEM.

A LITTLE way off the high road in Windsor — a nice farming town some ten miles from us — are Wahconah's Falls, in one of the most lonely and neglected spots in Berkshire. I had heard their praises eloquently spoken, by one who has an affinity for beauty, which searches out its kindred in all hidden nooks, and on a bracing Fall day I set out to visit them.

There are few drives through a more agreeable region. The village of Dalton, (Dale-town,) through which you pass, is a handsome town, with a fine old meeting-house on its ample, lawn-like green. You are enticed to linger, as well, by the dark, rushing river, where you see the groaning locomotive toiling wearily up the steep ascent above you. And there, too, the quaint looking paper mills, by the river side, go far to make up a pleasant and novel scene. It is said that as bright glances are sometimes thrown from the windows of these oddly shapen manufactories as from any balcony, lattice or verandah, whatever.

Leaving this pretty village, and its prettier belles, a few miles behind us we came to the Falls — a romantic miniature cataract — just far enough from the highway to be sheltered from the too careless eye. The eastern branch of the Housatonic here pours through perpendicular cliffs of grey marble a considerable volume of water, which in two or three sheets makes a descent of seventy or eighty feet. The scene is not very wild, but the dark precipitous cliffs form a striking and sombre vista, and the black and glassy surface of the water affords a fine contrast with the silvery white of the foam.

One may be sure of passing a pleasant hour at such a spot. The swift, smooth gliding of water always brings a pleasurable sensation, and there is rare music in the dash of a waterfall free from the discordant clatter of machinery. I confess to a malicious joy in looking upon the blackened ruins of an old mill which used to stand here, but perished long ago in some fierce combat with the insulted elements. Heaven send thee no successor, thou grim and grinning skeleton!

It is in such places as this, that sensible people cut up all manner of boyish antics. Never be over nice about dignity, when in search of the better thing, enjoyment; leave gravity and etiquette at home, in your wardrobe, with all other starched and flimsy articles of apparel. Get astride an island rock, that midway divides the stream, where the torrent shall throw its spray over you, and the current dash madly by, on either side your slippery foothold. Shout! rival the noisy stream at its own game. Notice now how superior is organic sound to any mere inarticulate noise. Your voice, lost in the thunder of the cataract so that you cannot hear your own words, comes out clear and distinct to your friends up on the shore. So the voice of true and prophetic genius, lost now in the mad roar of the multitude, shall ring its message in the ear of the listening future.

This cascade makes good its claim to be called beautiful, by gaining constantly on your affection. You come again, and again, to sit by its ebon pools, and let your eye glide with the fall of its glassy sheet, and sparkle with the glittering fragments into which it breaks among the rocks. I like these minor cataracts which do not oppress you with sublimity; where your soul is not absorbed by any awful grandeur. They are like those pleasant books where something is left for the imagination of the reader. There is room for the delights of an "if;" if it had been swollen to mighty bulk and curved like a horse shoe,—if it had been hung in air like the white ribbon of a bridal bonnet,—if it had fallen from so far that it had lost its way, and so on rainbow wings flown back to Heaven. Why, you have a whole cabinet of possible picturesques in that little germ.

There is a tradition about these Falls, which I received, years ago, from a young Indian of the civilized Stockbridge tribe, who had come from his exile in the Far West, to be educated at an Eastern college.

Wahconah.

At the close of the great Pequot War, in 1637, you recollect that the remnant of that gallant nation were driven out from Connecticut and dispersed over the land—as they touchingly said, "like the Autumn leaves, which the winds scatter and they return not, though the tree grow green again." In this sad exodus the great mass went to swell the tribes of the West; but a few bands chose to wander up the Housatonic to the valleys, where game was plenty and hunters were few. One of these small parties, under the lead of a young brave, called Miahcomo, built their frail village in that part of the valley now called Dalton. Here, for forty years, they lived in peace, and, begetting sons and daughters, increased in numbers far beyond the red man's wont. The hill-side, where they buried their dead; the glen, whose thick woods reflected the red glare of their council fire, became dear to them as home; but above all, the inaccessible mountains were prized, as the hunted man only can prize the strength of the hills.

Almost forty years had passed since the little tribe fled from the flames of Fort Mystic, when the great Sachem of the Wampanoags came to them. With strong logic, and glowing eloquence, he painted the rapid encroachments of the white man, and passionately besought them to join in that league which, in the following year, well nigh swept the English colonists from the soil of New England.

The young braves grasped their tomahawks as they listened, and the sympathetic eye of woman kindled with almost martial fire. But the rulers in savage, as in civilized life, can sometimes be prudent men. The chiefs crushed with cold words of sympathy the hopes which had quickened in the smiles of the people. Miahcomo — the same who led the tribe from the pursuit of the English — still ruled them; and the young warriors whispered that the horrors of the last night of

Fort Mystic, had turned his blood to water at the thought of the Long Knives — although bold as an eagle towards aught else. In more cautious tones they whispered, that if ever a spark of the old fire rekindled in Miahcomo's breast, the wily and cowardly priest Tashmu was always at hand to quench it. Thus the mission of Philip failed, and the tribe continued in peace.

In the early Summer, nearly two years after the visit of Philip, Miahcomo and his warriors were summoned to meet the Mohawks — to whom they had become feudatories — beyond the Taghconics. Trusting to the quiet of the valley, the village was left in charge of the women, and a few decrepit old men. Among the former was Wahconah, the old chief's favorite daughter, a young lady of singular personal attractions, and skilled in all the fine arts in vogue among her countrymen, — especially in that of angling. What with all these accomplishments, and the high rank of her father, it is little wonder that Wahconah was the idol of all the young men of the village; and, although yet almost a child in years, had — so the rumor ran — received offers matrimonial from a certain mysterious Mohawk dignitary. This latter worthy, the wigwam gossips unanimously agreed, would carry off the prize, whenever he came in person to claim it, — for it was a thing unheard of in Indian wooing, that a brave of fifty scalps should sue in vain.

The young gallants of the Housatonic did not, for all this, remit one whit of their attentions, so that, while they were over the border with her father, the hours hung heavily on the hands of Wahconah. It was, perhaps, to while away their tediousness; perhaps to get a nice dish for her lodge, that the maiden, one sunny afternoon in June, took her fishing lines and wandered up the river to our cascade. Before the sun went down her success had been abundant, and she only waited for one more last prize, — a habit which I notice is still invariable with successful people, be they anglers, speculators, or what not.

But Wahconah did not, after all, seem to have fully set her heart upon this final prize. On the contrary, she lay luxuriously back upon the soft greensward, playfully twining a few scarlet columbines in her dark hair, and smoothing softly down the gay feathers of the oriole and blue bird that decorated the edges of her white deer skin robe, — a garment which, it must be confessed, was rather excessive in its Bloomerism, considering the primitive nature of the wearer's pettiloons; but that was the fashion of the day, and no fault of Wahconah's.

The child-like maiden revelled in the very fullness of delightful idless. With a gentle, undisturbing thrill, she felt the richly colored clouds fill her with their delicious warmth; she dipped her little foot in the stream and laughed aloud to feel the soft caresses of the current; she mocked the blackbird that sung upon the oak, and the squirrel that chirped upon the hickory; she threw flowers and leaves upon the wave, and smiled maidenly when two chanced to meet and float together down the stream — for that was a love omen. That must have been a pleasant sight in the Summer twilight, almost two hundred years ago.

Pity if it had been lost! — as it was not, for all the while a young warrior had been looking on, from the shelter of a wood on the other side of the stream. It was certainly indelicate in him to play so long the spy upon a maiden's reveries, but one cannot find it in his heart to blame too severely, when he considers the temptation; and besides that, the offender was but a mere savage, and had never had the advantage of the counsels of Chesterfield, Abbot, or any "Young Man's Friend" whatever. The promptings of Nature, however, did at last suggest to him the impropriety of his course; or perhaps he grew impatient. At all events, he hailed Wahconah, in the flowery language of Indian gallantry, "Qua Alangua!" that is to say, "Hail! Bright Star!"

Wahconah, startled at the sudden appearance of a strange warrior, in the absence of her tribesmen, sprang to her feet; but preserving the calmness befitting Miacomo's daughter, replied, "Qua Sesah!" that is, "Hail! Brother!"

"Nessacus," continued the stranger, introducing himself, "Nessacus is weary with flying before the Long Knives, and his people faint by the way. Will the Bright Star's people shut their lodges against their brethren?"

"Miahcomo has gone toward the setting sun," replied the maiden, — who by this time had probably come to the conclusion that Nessacus was a very handsome young man, and well behaved, — "but his lodges are always open. Let my brother's people follow, and be welcome."

A signal from the young chief brought a weary, travel-worn band to his side, and Wahconah led the way to the village, while Nessacus related to her the sad story of Philip's defeat and death. "They waste us," he said, "as the pestilence which forerun them wasted our fathers."

"The Manitou is angry with his red children," said Wahconah; He makes the white man mighty, by the strength of the long knife and the fire bird."

"It is not that," responded her companion bitterly, "but the traitor's tongue at our council fires, and the traitor's arrow upon our war path."

Wahconah remembered what the people whispered concerning Tashmu, and was silent. Thus they came to the village, — but I am not writing a tale, and must let pass the welcome, and the house keeping, as well, until Miahcomo's return. Suffice it that, in those pleasant days of the Moon of Flowers, the young people did just what you and I would have been likely to do, — that is, fell violently in love; and, what was more, in direct violation of Indian customs, told each other so,— a breach of etiquette you will the more readily pardon, if you know experimentally, (as I doubt not you do,) how dementing is the glance of a bright eye, and the bloom of a damask cheek, in the soft light of a June evening, when your heart is as full of love as the air is of fragrance.

Four suns had ripened the passion of our new lovers, and a fifth was shining genially upon it, when a messenger came in, announcing the near approach of Miahcomo; and, as the custom was, all the people went out to meet him. What visions of happiness our dreamers had built up, in their barbarous way, I cannot tell; nor do I know whether Indian sires have such a fatal way of laying siege to air castles as more civilized fathers use; so you can guess, as well as I, whether any tremblings troubled the hearts of our young friends, akin to what young 'Squire Mansfield and old Banker Barker's daughter might experience, in corresponding circumstances. But remember, one love is very much like another.

Wahconah and the chief of her guests stood together, as, just up the valley, the returning warriors came in sight. Their leader is described as a fine old hero as one should desire to see. His tall, sinewy frame was scarcely bent by the snows of seventy Winters; every wrinkle in his face was firm as if it were a new sinew of added strength; his eye keen and piercing as that of his youngest archer.

By the chief's side walked a different figure, meek even to cringing, with an uncertain step, and weak, restless, unquiet eye. It was the priest Tashmu,—one of that strange cast often hated, sometimes despised, but always feared by the aborigines. This Tashmu was a constant attendant upon Miahcomo, and, it was said, had acquired a strange and mysterious power over the chief's mind.

Wahconah shrank from the presence of the wizard, as the Summer flower shrinks from the north wind; but his was not now the most unwelcome figure in the approaching band. With her father and the priest came a burly warrior, not positively old, nor absolutely ugly — only a little smoke dried or so, and marked by certain transverse and obverse scars, which, although doubtless very honorable, might have been dispensed with as mere matters of ornament. He was evidently a man of renown, and wore the scalps, that hung dangling about him, as proudly as ever a civilized hero his jewelled star or blushing ribbon. Wahconah guessed, but too shrewdly, that this was her Mohawk lover, — although he was far too dignified a character to conduct his wooing in the unceremonious manner of his young rival. Perhaps it had been but awkward work had he tried it.

When the parties met, a few words explained to the chief why the strangers were his guests, and ensured a ratification of his daughter's welcome. Whatever may have been his meditations upon learning the disasters of his race, they did not prevent his holding high revel that night, upon the banks of the Housatonic. Feasts were celebrated, and games held, in honor at once of all his guests. I leave you to guess whose eyes brightened as Nessacus carried off all the prizes for daring feats and skillful, and whose darkened as the brawny arms and square frame of the Mohawk, Yonnongah, excelled all, in their marvellous strength. There was yet another eye, stealthily and intently watching every glance and action, and divining the thoughts of careless hearts, for Tashmu was already the enemy of the young exile.

Nessacus was no laggard in love nor in business. Early on the morning after the feast, he repaired to the lodge of Miahcomo, and the two remained long in conference. The visit was again and again repeated, but still the nature of their business did not transpire; only the name of Wahconah was mixed in the gossip about it, and it was surmised that the suit of the Mohawk was, perhaps, getting in a bad way. The young chief was certainly getting to be a favorite of the old.

But the power of the Mohawk, and the craft of the priest, were at work; and they were dangerous enemies. It was the part of the latter to unearth the game; to discover and bring the plans of Nessacus into open day, where his ally could attack them. He succeeded; two propositions soon came to be national affairs, for the discussion of the council fire — the first for the marriage of Wahconah with Nessacus, and the second for the migration of the tribe to the West, beyond the reach of the white man's encroachments. To the first Miahcomo gave his support — but he clung to the spot where he had ruled so long and so prosperously.

On the other hand, Yonnongah demanded the maiden for his fourth wife, on the strength of some ancient promise of her father, and denounced the vengeance of his nation if their tributaries should attempt to migrate beyond their jurisdiction. Yonnongah seemed bent upon securing Wahconah, alternately employing threats and those sweet promises, of which even an Indian lover can be so profuse, — especially after having already won three hearts. This was no matter of jest with the sorely perplexed father and chief, for Yonnongah was a man of might in his nation, and would have scant scruples of delicacy in fulfilling his threats. All which Tashmu lost no occasion of urging upon the chief, to the great detriment of our hero's cause.

Nessacus soon saw how matters were tending, and, conscious of his inability to cope with the priest in his own arts, took a bold, blunt man's way of settling the matter, and challenged his rival to decide the disputes by arms. Yonnongah, who, to do him justice, was a brave man, closed at once with the proposal; but the priest was not thus to be cheated of his chance of villany. Signs and portents multiplied marvellously; not a bird could fly, or a fish swim, or a cloud float, but each was pregnant with a prohibition of the proposed combat. The powers above and below combined to forbid it. The thunder muttered the divine veto; the winds breathed it; the stars winked it. If you could believe Tashmu, never was such a commotion in Heaven, and "elsewhere," as the coming duel had raised. The trial by arms was abandoned.

It was but fair, since the gods had vetoed one mode of solving the difficulty, that they should provide another. So thought Tashmu, and exclaimed in the council, "Let the Great Spirit speak."

"Let us obey the will of the Great Spirit," responded Miahcomo reverently.

And Yonnongah said, "It is well."

It was then proclaimed that Tashmu would, by divination, enquire that night in the "Wizard's Glen" how the will of the Manitou should be ascertained; and a "bad spell" was denounced against all who went beyond the precincts of the village, while he was engaged in his holy work. Many predicted ill to Nessacus, from this committal of his fate to the hands of a known enemy, but none ventured to remonstrate against the decree.

A few rods below the cataract at Wahconah's Falls is a sharp rock, which divides the stream. At the time of our tradition, the current flowed equally upon either side of it, and it had often been used, like the flight of birds, the aspect of clouds, and other simple objects in nature, to ascertain the will of Heaven. Upon the night of Tashmu's supposed divination in the "Wizzard's Glen," that respectable minister of religion might, instead, have been seen here, assisted by the stronger arms of his Mohawk friend, tugging away at certain great rocks which lay near the shore, and which they finally contrived to place in the water, so as to impede the current upon one side.

At this same spot, by the river side, a day or two afterwards, the tribe were assembled, and it was announced to them that Manitou had delegated the Spirit of the Stream to settle their difficulties. In other words — a small canoe, curiously carved with mysterious hieroglyphics, was to be launched midway in the river, and, as the current chanced to carry it on one side or the other of the dividing rock, the questions in dispute were to be decided. This was a mode of solving knotty points by no means uncommon, and which, therefore, excited no surprise, except that the Priest's chances for trickery seemed to be lessened. Simple souls! who knew not that what appears the fairest field often affords the best harvest to accomplished knaves!

An "era of good feeling" seemed now to dawn. All parties hastened to adopt this as a "finality." Tashmu, in oily words, wished well to his brother Nessacus; and Nessacus resigned himself, unreservedly, to the care of his brother Tashmu. The Priest was as much puzzled as pleased, at this sudden access of confidence; but it, at least, made his part easy to play.

A solemn feast was now held; and the magical bark, freighted with so many hopes, was then poised in the middle of the stream. Miahcomo was placed, in savage state, at a conspicuous point, while Yonnongah and his rival were assigned separate sides of the river.

"Let Manitou speak!" exclaimed the Priest; and the sacred canoe, released from its moorings, floated steadily down the stream — inclining now to the right hand, now to the left. All eyes intently followed its course, hardly doubting that, by some charm or other, Tashmu would at last cause it to pass near Yonnongah. You will guess that none counted more confidently on such a result than that worthy himself. Still the bark floated regardlessly on, until it touched the magic rock, — hung poised there for a moment, then seemed to incline toward the Mohawk; but, the inconstant current striking it obliquely, it swung slowly round, as upon a pivot, and passed down the stream, by the feet of Nessacus.

"Wagh! the Great Spirit hath spoken, and it is good!" exclaimed Miahcomo; and the people, whose hearts the young chief had somehow gained, shouted "Ho! It is good!"

The Priest and his accomplice gazed at each other in silent astonishment, that Heaven could possibly decide against arguments of such weight as they had used. The former, for a moment, began to suspect that a great God might possibly, in reality, rule in the affairs of men, — making him to bless whom he would have cursed. But the idea was too mighty for him, and he recurred, naturally, to a suspicion of treachery. I need not say, however, that he had his own reasons for not pressing an immediate investigation. I do not know that it ever occurred to him that Nessacus might have been a witness to his pious midnight labors, and, improving upon the hint, rendered them abortive.

The assent of all parties was accordingly given to the proposed marriage; and the time which intervened between the trial and a "lucky day," was to be filled up with feasting and revelry. The disappearance of Tashmu from the scene added to the hilarity of the occasion, and all was wild merriment.

But alarming intelligence interrupted their festivities. The terrible Major Tallcott, with his soldiers, had pursued the brave Sachem of Quaboag across the mountains, and slain him, with more than two score of his best warriors, at Mahaiwe, on the banks of the Housatonic, not thirty miles from the settlement of Miahcomo. Even their temporary security was gone; the mountain barrier was already passed.

The fugitives from the battle at Mahaiwe came thronging in, but at last brought intelligence that the invaders had returned. A party of them brought, also, the missing Tashmu, whom they accused of having offered to lead the enemy to the refuge of Nessacus. The evidence of his guilt was complete, and the fate of the criminal was not delayed by any unnecessary judicial forms.

Only a want of provisions had prevented Major Tallcott from accepting the Wizard's kind offer, and he might now return, at any moment, to profit by it. The best haste was accordingly made in their migration, and before the November winds blew, Nessacus had led them to a home in the West, where they became a great tribe, and flourished for many generations, before they again heard the white man's rifle.

As for Wahconah, the story of her happiness comes down to us, through Indian traditions, faint and far, but sweet as the perfume which a western gale might bring from a far-off prairie.

THE END.

www.ingramcontent.com/pod-product-compliance
Lightning Source LLC
LaVergne TN
LVHW050529100826
845148LV00002B/486

* 9 7 8 1 4 2 5 5 1 9 3 5 3 *